MENCIUS

Translations from the Asian Classics

MENCIUS

Translated by Irene Bloom

EDITED AND WITH AN INTRODUCTION
BY PHILIP J. IVANHOE

Columbia University Press
New York

Columbia University Press
Publishers Since 1893
New York   Chichester, West Sussex

Copyright © 2009 Columbia University Press
Paperback edition, 2011
All rights reserved

Library of Congress Cataloging-in-Publication Data
Mencius.
[Mengzi. English.]
Mencius / translated by Irene Bloom ;
edited and with an introduction by Philip J. Ivanhoe.
p. cm. — (Translations from the Asian Classics)
Includes index.
ISBN 978-0-231-12204-7 (cloth)—ISBN 978-0-231-12205-4 (pbk)— ISBN 978-0-231-52058-4
(ebook)
I. Bloom, Irene.   II. Ivanhoe, P. J.   III. Title.   V. Series.

PL2478.P24   2009
181'.112—dc22   2009005319

CONTENTS

Jennifer Crewe, of Columbia University Press, asked me to edit Professor Irene T. Bloom's manuscript translation of *Mencius* and to write an introduction in order to finish the work that illness prevented Professor Bloom from completing. I have done my best to preserve not only the meaning but also the spirit of Professor Bloom's translation, making only a few minor changes in passages where I am confident she would have been persuaded to change her mind had we the chance to discuss matters. I have added a few additional references and Chinese characters in places where she indicated some significant interpretive or textual issue had informed her translation. In editing the text, I had the good fortune of being guided by a set of splendid comments by Professor Burton Watson; his helpful suggestions aided me greatly and enhanced the final product significantly.

I am honored to have had the chance to assist a colleague and friend like Irene Bloom. Her work, on both *Mencius* and neo-Confucian thinkers, her example, and her counsel have influenced me since I was in graduate school. I feel most fortunate to have known such an insightful, generous, patient, sensitive, and elegant scholar. I know I shall not look upon her like again and hope that some of her likeness comes through in this work.

Philip J. Ivanhoe
City University of Hong Kong

The Man and the Work

Mencius records the teachings of the Chinese philosopher whose surname was Meng 孟 and personal name Ke 軻. Throughout East Asia, he is better known as Mengzi 孟子, or "Master Meng" (391–308 B.C.E.); "Mencius" is the Latinized version of this more widely used appellation. Mencius lived during the later part of the Zhou dynasty (traditional dates: 1122–249 B.C.E.), in a time known as the Warring States period (403–221 B.C.E.). This was an age in which the older feudal order of the Zhou dynasty had deteriorated. The Zhou king ruled in name only and his former empire was divided into different states, each with its own ruler, who continued to vie with the rulers of other states for supremacy. These state rulers often illegitimately claimed for themselves the title of king (*wang* 王) in an attempt to arrogate to themselves what rightfully belonged to the now enfeebled Zhou king. These features of Mencius's time often are reflected in the conversations he had with rulers of various states, for example his conversations with King Hui of Liang and King Xuan of Qi in the first part of book 1, about how they might realize their grand ambition to unite and rule over all of China. As readers will see from the translation, Mencius thought that only someone who possessed the moral qualities of a true king, someone *worthy* of the title, could successfully unify the empire, and in many of his conversations he tries to steer the attention of various state rulers from their desire for power to a concern with morality. Like Kongzi (Confucius) before him, Mencius defended the older Zhou form of life, which of course entailed the preeminence of the Zhou king, but he did so in a new, intellectually more diverse and sophisticated context. He faced a wide range of formidable challengers to the Way (*dao* 道) Confucius had advocated—see for example 3A4, 3A5, 3B9, 6A1–6, and 7A26—and in response to their contending theories and ideas he developed innovative, powerful, and highly nuanced views about human nature, the mind, self-cultivation, politics, and Heaven that had a profound and lasting influence on the later Confucian tradition and on East Asian culture in general.

Mencius lived in Zou 鄒, a small state located at the base of what is now the Shandong Peninsula. Tradition claims that he studied under Confucius's grandson Zisi 子思, but it is more likely that he was a student of one of Zisi's disciples. One piece of evidence supporting the claim of a connection to Zisi is the fact that some of Mencius's teachings bear similarities to parts of the *Doctrine of the Mean*, which is traditionally ascribed to Zisi. Recently excavated texts also reveal a number of common themes, which show us more clearly the extent to which Mencius was participating in contemporary philosophical debates and helping to shape the emerging Confucian tradition.[1]

The earliest information we have about Mencius's life comes from the text that bears his name; later, this picture of his life was substantially augmented though not revised by his biography in Sima Qian's 司馬遷 *The Grand Scribe's Records* (*Shiji* 史記), which was composed in the early part of the first century B.C.E.[2] In its present form, *Mencius* consists of seven books, each of which is divided into two parts, which are further subdivided into sections of varying length. This general structure is followed in Professor Bloom's translation, with each book, part, and section assigned a number or letter. For example, section 7 in the first part of book 1 is 1A7, while section 15 of the second part of book 6 is 6B15. The shortest sections of the text consist of brief dicta, while the longest are quite substantial. These passages purportedly record the teachings of Mencius and conversations he had with various disciples, friends, royal patrons, and rivals. Some traditional accounts claim that Mencius himself composed the original text, others say it was compiled by his disciples with his approval and advice. In the second century C.E., *Mencius* underwent a significant transformation when it was edited and several "chapters" were discarded by Zhao Qi 趙歧 (d. 201 C.E.), who also wrote the first extant commentary on the text.

Mencius had a place, though not a commanding position, among Confucian writings until its extraordinary ascent. This began toward the end of the Tang dynasty (618–907), when thinkers such as Han Yu 韓愈 (768–824) and Li Ao 李翱 (fl. 798) advocated *Mencius* as a particularly important resource for the revival of Confucianism, which had fallen into relative neglect in the face of a remarkable and rising tide of Daoist and Buddhist innovation and success.[3] In the following, Song dynasty (960–1279), the inimitable Zhu Xi 朱熹 (1130–1200) wrote a highly influential commentary on *Mencius* and included the latter, along with the *Analects, Great Learning*, and *Doctrine of the Mean*, as one of the *Four Books*—a collection that came to serve as the gateway to Confucian learning and the all-important civil service examination. Largely as a result of these developments, in subsequent dynasties *Mencius* came to occupy a singularly important place in the Confucian scriptural pantheon. In 1315, the Mongol court recognized it as a classic, which secured its preeminent position within the tradition; since that time the text has enjoyed unprecedented and unmatched influence and prestige. Among current scholars, it remains one of the most highly studied Confucian classics.

Ethical Views

Mencius's primary ethical concern, both theoretical and practical, was moral self-cultivation; he wanted people to improve themselves and believed they could do so with the right kind of attitude and effort.[4] Like many Confucians, he was more a teacher or therapist than a theoretician, more interested in moving people toward a certain ideal than in crafting and presenting tight and careful valid arguments. This is not to say that he does not present interesting and at times compelling arguments, only that this was not his aim or ideal. Readers should keep in mind his more practical concerns as they seek to gain a sympathetic understanding of his philosophy and life.

At the core of Mencius's theory of self-cultivation is a belief in the innate moral qualities and inclination of human nature. He is best known for his theory that human nature is good (*xing shan* 性善), and readers will find him discussing this topic in a variety of places in the text, most notably but by no means exclusively in the opening sections of the first part of book 6. Mencius meant by this claim, first, that human beings possess certain observable and active resources for becoming good, what he calls moral "sprouts." In more modern terms, we might describe this part of his view as the claim that human beings innately possess some measure of other-regarding desires such as compassion and altruism.[5] In addition, Mencius argues that if human beings exercise the most important and distinctive aspects of their nature—for example, their innate moral sensibilities and their abilities to reflect and think—according to what he regards as their natural functions, this will lead them to develop their moral sprouts into full and vibrant virtues. The key to this process of development is the mind (*xin* 心), an organ Mencius believed contained affective, cognitive, and volitional elements.[6] Roughly, his view is that if we exercise our minds and reflect upon ourselves and our condition, we will discover not only that we do in fact care about other people, creatures, and things, but also that focusing upon our moral sprouts leads us to act morally and offers us the most profound, stable, and enduring sources of satisfaction available to creatures like us. This satisfaction or joy in moral action, along with a parallel sense of disapproval and shame in bad action, can lead us to become good, but only if we exercise our minds to reflect upon and follow the "greater part" of our nature (6A15).

There are numerous challenges one might raise to Mencius's position as a moral view for our time. Even if one grants most of what he claims about the relationship between nature and moral development, one can still question *why* one should follow one's nature. What gives normative status and power to the promptings of our nature and its development through reflection? Mencius's most direct and explicit answer was religious in nature: Heaven granted us our nature, and coming to understand and develop our nature is the way to understand and accord with the will of Heaven. We will explore these claims and other aspects of Mencius's religious views in the following section, but even if we set them aside, there are other possible ways to defend a version of Mencius's position, several of which he appeals to, though does not fully develop.

One might begin a defense of Mencius's views by noting that simply by raising the questions of why one should be moral or what morality is, one implicitly endorses the view that human beings are by nature creatures that *reflect* upon themselves and their actions and seek answers with their minds. This supports his claim that the natural function of the mind is to think or reflect and help us govern our lives. Mencius would further insist that not only are we reflective creatures but also that many of our reflections include evaluations and spontaneous responses to what we or others have done or are considering doing. On its own, this point seems quite uncontroversial, though of course Mencius would have to go on to show that certain kinds of responses are characteristic of normal, well-informed human beings and do indeed produce a profound and particularly valuable sense of satisfaction and joy.[7] If one reads Mencius as offering a form of virtue ethics or a broadly construed version of consequentialism, such claims about the true character of human nature can contribute in direct and important ways to a plausible ethical theory.[8] For if following and developing certain parts of our nature are critical for producing a stable and harmonious society of satisfied and joyful people, the value of understanding the true character and potential of human nature clearly plays a prominent and critical role in both ethical theory and practice.

Political Views

Mencius was one of the first thinkers in the history of the world to insist that rulers and states exist to serve their people. The proper aim of a good state is the welfare of its people, and this is conceived in terms of the order, security, wealth, happiness, and education the people enjoy. Mencius believed the people are the only tangible indicator of good governance, and elite members of society must look to the people as the most reliable gauge of the quality of their rule and heed what this guide reveals. Much to the chagrin of the rulers in his own time and a number of later Chinese emperors as well, Mencius further argued that rulers who fail to serve their people lose the mandate to rule and can even be forcibly removed by those more qualified to fulfill Heaven's plan for its people.[9] These forceful and at times quite subtle views about the role the welfare of the people plays in justifying political rule did not include any clear correlates to Western ideas about a right to revolt or to elect those who govern. Nevertheless, Mencius's views about the wisdom and importance of the people have the potential to significantly enrich present-day political philosophy.[10]

Like Confucius before him, Mencius offered nuanced and interest-ing ideas on what *constitutes* the welfare of the people. His views about the importance of family and intimate interpersonal relationships call for very different approaches to how one conceives of and seeks to en-sure basic welfare. Like any Confucian, Mencius would adamantly re-ject the idea that simply providing for the material needs of people is in any way adequate. To treat someone in such a fashion is to treat that person as less than fully human.[11] Confucians also place a tremendous emphasis on education as a chief concern of the government and a pri-mary good for the people. One can see a number of ways in which a good education, and especially one with ethical content, can contribute both directly and indirectly to a person's welfare and to the welfare of the state as well and why it arguably should be one of the highest pri-orities of any decent society.

A number of current thinkers have focused on Mencius's views about human nature as a resource for developing Confucian concep-tions of human rights.[12] While one does not find an explicit discus-sion of rights or even clear cases of the concept of rights in the early Confucian tradition,[13] Mencius's belief in a common, ethically charged nature unambiguously establishes what Donald J. Munro calls natural equality among human beings.[14] Throughout the early tradition, one also finds the notion that human beings all are regarded by and can ap-peal to Heaven to bear testimony to their moral worth, no matter how badly they might be treated by others. These ideas offer a clear and solid foundation for developing a robust conception of basic rights.

Early Confucians describe a system of moral right and wrong, good and bad largely in terms of a set of virtues and a system of rituals and norms. These function to achieve many of the same goods as a system of rights and laws. Nevertheless, Confucians emphasize being humane (*ren* 仁) rather than the modern Western notion of justice. They clearly have a concept of justice, in terms of what is due to a person given her or his social role and circumstance and simply in virtue of being a fellow human being, but their sense of justice is distinctive and needs to be carefully distinguished from its modern Western counterparts.[15] As Munro has shown, early Confucians most definitely have a sense of equal human worth and dignity, clear views about the ability to make and adhere to moral choices, and to take on and assign blame, praise, and responsibility. Together, these and other ethical ideas and practices constitute a distinctively Confucian way of life that is importantly different from the modern Western liberal view. Roughly, one might say that people have dignity and moral worth because of their innate moral nature, as members of families and a larger society, and because they possess the capacity to develop themselves to be good, and so forth.[16]

Those who argue that Confucianism *cannot* develop any robust conception of rights almost certainly are wrong. To make such a case, one would have to show that the tradition is unable to adapt, develop, and change. Anyone who has made even the slightest effort to study, understand, and appreciate the rich, creative, and still vibrant history of Confucianism will find such a claim both naive and implausible; like all great traditions, Confucianism has demonstrated a remarkable ability to transform *itself* as well as those who participate in it. The view that Confucianism is somehow incapable of developing or accommodating any conception of rights must recognize that, for most of its history, the Western tradition lacked any robust sense of basic rights. The notions of rights, autonomy, and free will all are modern developments. Unless one can show that such developments could only take *one unique route*, there is no conceptual reason that prevents the Confucian tradition—or the Daoist, Buddhist, and Hindu traditions—from following its own path to a related or largely similar idea. I suggest, however, that rather than simply looking to find, develop, or apply the modern Western liberal notion of rights within the Confucian tradition, we might all best be served by working to describe an alternative Confucian foundation and conception of rights. Surely this would be better than groping for some weak conception of rights within traditional culture, as some have done, or seeking to graft onto a vital and rich tradition an alien and unfamiliar ideal. Seen in this light, the Confucian tradition, and Mencius's philosophy in particular, have tremendous potential for contributing to and enhancing our understanding of the notion of human rights.

Mencius's views on war also are incisive and immensely interesting. He offered clear and intriguing views about all three of the standard concerns one finds in modern Western just-war traditions: *jus ad bellum, jus in bello,* and *jus post bellum.*[17] His views on war were deeply informed and shaped by his central concern with benevolence and the welfare of the people, which places considerable restrictions on when and how a state can go to war and what it owes its own and other people in the aftermath of war. One intriguing consequence of Mencius's theory is described in 1B15, where he recounts the story of a king who could find no way to appease or defend against an alien aggressor and who, in response, chose to abdicate his throne and leave his state in order to avoid pointlessly harming his people.

Mencius's views about just war continue to play a central and vital role in current Chinese conceptions of and responses to war. When the United States launched its second war with Iraq, there was widespread condemnation in the Chinese media, especially on the Internet. The most common criticism of the American action drew upon the distinction Mencius describes in passages such as 1A5, 1B11, 7B2, and 7B4 between a campaign of justified punishment (*zheng* 征) and acts of interstate aggression. Many Chinese regarded the first Gulf War as a case of the former but saw the second war as a clear example of the latter.

Religious Views

It is still not uncommon to find present-day scholars claiming that early Confucians such as Confucius and Mencius are agnostic or purely secular thinkers. Such claims, though, are not supported by the texts.[18] As noted, Heaven plays an important role in Mencius's ethical philosophy. Like Confucius before him, Mencius believed that Heaven has a plan for human beings, both individually and collectively, and is conscious of, interested in, and on occasion plays a part in the unfolding of human affairs. Also like Confucius, Mencius believed that Heaven had chosen *him* to play a special part in the realization of its grand design.

Mencius, though, changed the focus and altered the content of Confucius's earlier views about Heaven. This is seen most clearly in Mencius's teachings concerning human nature. He explicitly claimed that Heaven endowed human beings with a nature that both equips and inclines them toward the goals that it has in mind for them. Because human beings have such a distinctive nature, they have a direct way of coming to understand and follow Heaven. By reflecting upon their nature, people can come to understand not only themselves but also the proper role all human beings are to play in the grand plan Heaven has for the world. In 7A1, Mencius teaches that a proper understanding of human nature leads to an understanding of Heaven and that working to develop one's nature fully is the way to serve Heaven.

Mencius's views about Heaven place significant constraints on the nature of the human good. Human beings are to seek for satisfaction, joy, harmony, and general well-being *within* a natural order established by Heaven. Much, though not all, of Heaven's plan can be known through careful reflection and study; with enough effort of the right kind, human beings can come to understand, but they must not attempt to alter or fundamentally damage the order provided by Heaven, for to do so would violate Heaven's plan.

If one were to ignore or seek to eliminate the religious aspects of Mencius's thought, it would alter the character of his philosophy.[19] Without Heaven, Mencius's claims about the goodness of human nature would not only lose a sense of being part of a much greater good, they would become a much more open-ended quest for what is good for creatures like us. Many would agree that greater openness on this issue should be welcomed. If, however, one eliminates all sense of a natural order and embraces efforts to alter both human nature and the world around us in fundamental ways, in a search for greater satisfaction and happiness, Mencius's defenders might argue, and compellingly so, that one is no longer searching for the *human* good; rather, one is stipulating and working to manufacture a new order for oneself and the world. Such an attitude toward morality begs important questions, perhaps most important is whether morality is made for human beings or human beings are made—or, on this view, remade—for morality.

Wider Influence on Culture

Mencius's influence on Chinese culture extends far beyond his contributions to ethical, political, and religious thought, impressive as they are. His example as a defender of Confucianism and Chinese culture in general was an important reason he and his ideas proved to have such a remarkable legacy. Mencius was the first thinker to defend Confucius's Way against a range of articulate challengers. In so doing, he established a precedent and inspiring example that later Confucians would follow and explicitly appeal to throughout the history of the tradition. Later thinkers often invoke the trope of *being forced* to respond to, challenge, and oppose some new threat to the Confucian tradition and Chinese society; they thus cast themselves as latter-day versions of Mencius, who, we are told, far from being "fond of argument," was "compelled" to engage in it in order to defend the Way (3B9).

Another reason *Mencius* has endured and exerted such a profound influence on Chinese culture is its remarkable literary qualities. It is one of the most elegant and accessible classical Chinese texts and abounds with memorable and clever stories, powerful and at times haunting images, and wonderful turns of phrase. It is an abundant source for the distinctive feature of the Chinese language called set phrases (*cheng yu* 成語): expressions, usually of four characters, still used in modern oral and written Chinese to invoke complex ideas in terse yet highly evocative and often amusing ways. For example, the phrase "climbing a tree in search of a fish" (*yuan shu qiu yu* 緣樹求魚) is from 1A7 and is used to describe actions that are hopeless and wrongheaded; the phrase "pulling at the sprouts to help them grow" (*ba miao zhu zhang* 拔苗助長) is from 2A2 and describes actions that foolishly aim to rush a natural process and as a result harm the cause one seeks to advance. Simply by invoking these four-character expressions, speakers or authors conjure up and continue parts of the rich Mencian legacy.

Stories about Mencius's mother have added wisdom and luster to his reputation as well.[20] Such stories fill out a picture, whether historically accurate or not, that has influenced people's image of and admiration for not only his mother but Mencius as well. Most of the stories describe Mencius's mother displaying her remarkable wisdom and virtue through a variety of actions and advice. Most famous is the story of how "Mencius's mother moved three times" (*Meng mu san qian* 孟母三遷), which is captured in another set phrase, known to people throughout East Asia. The story goes that Mencius's mother, a young widow left to raise her son, changed their residence three times. They first lived next to a cemetery, but she was not pleased to see her son mimic the actions of those performing funeral rituals. So she moved near a market, but then was not wholly satisfied when young Mencius would imitate the actions and words of those hawking goods. Determined to find the best possible environment for her son, she moved a third time, settling down and finding contentment near a school, where her son intoned the lessons of teachers and followed their example of diligent study. This is but one of several highly memorable stories about the insight and determination of Mencius's mother and how she guided and shaped her son's education and moral development. These tales offer powerful ideals and vivid images—which often have been depicted in popular illustrations—that inspire many "education mothers" throughout East Asian civilization and beyond; they represent another important facet of Mencius's influence upon and enduring legacy within Chinese and East Asian culture.

A final and more amorphous influence is no less real or important, and that is the powerful current of humanity running throughout Chinese culture. Mencius's view of human nature and its potential for good has penetrated deeply and resides in the marrow and bones of the Chinese people; it finds expression in a wide range of cultural phenomena. There is an often unexpressed imperative echoing down through Chinese history calling on every person, from the most powerful to the most humble, to cultivate and manifest fundamental decency, kindness, and ethical nobility.[21] Whereas people in Western culture tend to reserve the worst approbation for those who are unjust, the Chinese reserve such condemnation for those who are uncaring or unfeeling, and there is something to their preference. The latter ideal is more within any person's ability, and failing on this standard may well show a more fundamental lack of one of the most basic and cherished qualities of human beings. We in the West seem to share something like this view as well, at least in our more popular appraisals—think of the character Scrooge—and after all, we use the word *humanity* both to designate ourselves as a species and to describe one of our best qualities. In any event, Mencius was the first to sound this call and illustrate it with moving parables such as King Xuan sparing the ox (1A7), the story of the child and the well (2A6), and the desolation of Ox Mountain (6A8).

Mencius's irrepressibly optimistic appraisal of human nature and his endorsement of the human spirit are perhaps the greatest legacy of his philosophy; the fact that most Chinese people and many scholars of Chinese culture would simply call these ideas *Confucian* or *Chinese* only testifies to the degree to which his ideas have permeated this magnificent civilization and East Asian cultures more generally. With the publication of works like this translation by Irene Bloom, the Mencian legacy continues to grow and spread beyond China and East Asia, to find sympathetic readers in the English-speaking world. This is only fitting, for Mencius did not write just for the Chinese but for all human beings; his message was never aimed at any single person, people, or state; it was intended and belongs to what he called all-under-Heaven (*tian xia* 天下).

Philip J. Ivanhoe

Notes

1. For an excellent introduction to this material that carefully traces some of the most important connections to Mencius's philosophy, see Mark Csikszentmihalyi, *Material Virtue: Ethics and the Body in Early China* (Leiden: Brill, 2004).

2. For an account of Mencius's early life and sources describing his life, see the "Life of Mencius" section of the "Prolegomena" in James Legge, trans., *The Works of Mencius* (repr., New York: Dover, 1970), 14–38; and appendixes 1 and 2 in D. C. Lau, trans., *Mencius* (London: Penguin, 1970), 205–19.

3. The degree to which later Confucians altered Mencius's philosophy, knowingly or unknowingly, and the ways in which his thought informed neo-Confucian reflection constitute a complex and controversial matter. For a study that focuses on the appropriation of Mencius's philosophy by a highly influential Ming-dynasty philosopher, see Philip J. Ivanhoe, *Ethics in the Confucian Tradition: The Thought of Mengzi and Wang Yangming*, 2nd ed. (Indianapolis: Hackett, 2002).

4. There are a number of works and anthologies dedicated to Mencius's philosophy; among the most helpful are Kwong-loi Shun, *Mencius and Early Chinese Thought* (Stanford, Calif.: Stanford University Press, 1997); Liu Xiusheng and Philip J. Ivanhoe, eds., *Essays on Mencius's Moral Philosophy* (Indianapolis: Hackett, 2002); and Alan K. L. Chan, ed., *Mencius: Contexts and Interpretations* (Honolulu: University of Hawai'i Press, 2002).

5. For a critical defense of this aspect of Mencius's view from the perspective of evolutionary biology, see Donald J. Munro, *A Chinese Ethics for the New Century* (Hong Kong: Chinese University Press, 2005), 47–87.

6. These features of the *xin* have led a number of modern-day authors to translate the term as "heart-mind" or "heart-and-mind." I follow Professor Bloom's choice of "mind" in this introduction.

7. The most plausible version of such an argument would employ counterfactual and not merely empirical appeals.

8. For a revealing, current exploration of these issues, see Bryan W. van Norden, *Virtue Ethics and Consequentialism in Early Chinese Philosophy* (New York: Cambridge University Press, 2007).

9. Emperor Hong Wu (1368–1398) was so displeased by these aspects of Mencius's philosophy that he had passages dealing with these themes excised from the text. The Japanese court was not only unhappy but outraged by these parts of *Mencius*. For a discussion of these responses to Mencius's political views, see Ivanhoe, *Ethics in the Confucian Tradition*, 176, n. 36.

10. For a splendid discussion of Mencius's views about the role of the people in legitimating rule, see Justin Tiwald, "A Right of Rebellion in the *Mengzi*?" *Dao: A Journal of Comparative Philosophy* 7, no. 3 (Fall 2008): 269–82.

11. For an excellent modern treatment of Confucian views on welfare, see Joseph Chan, "Giving Priority to the Worst-Off: A Confucian Perspective on Social Welfare," in *Confucianism for the Modern World*, ed. Daniel A. Bell and Hahm Chaibong, 236–53 (New York: Cambridge University Press, 2003). For an account of how Confucian values place limits on property rights, see Daniel A. Bell, "Confucian Constraints on Property Rights," in ibid., 218–35.

12. A seminal work on this topic is Irene T. Bloom, "Fundamental Intuitions and Consensus Statements: Mencian Confucianism and Human Rights," in *Confucianism and Human Rights*, ed. Wm. Theodore de Bary and Tu Weiming, 94–116 (New York: Columbia University Press, 1998). For a defense of the resources within the Chinese tradition for developing and defending a conception of rights, see Wm. Theodore de Bary, *Asian Values and Human Rights: A Confucian Communitarian Perspective* (Cambridge, Mass.: Harvard University Press, 1998). For a historically informed comparative study, see Stephen C. Angle, *Human Rights and Chinese Thought: A Cross-Cultural Inquiry* (New York: Cambridge University Press, 2002). For a collection of original material focused on the topic of rights, see Stephen C. Angle and Marina Svensson, eds., *The Chinese Human Rights Reader: Documents and Commentary* (Armonk, N.Y.: M. E. Sharpe, 2001).

13. See Tiwald's article, cited in n. 10, for a careful study that illustrates the need to work through the texts with care and philosophical sophistication.

14. Donald J. Munro, *The Concept of Man in Early China* (Stanford, Calif.: Stanford University Press, 1969), 1–22. Munro very helpfully distinguishes this "natural equality" from "evaluative equality," which concerns equal achievement of moral character in contrast to a shared natural endowment.

15. For an insightful and revealing exploration of the distinctive concept and sense of justice one finds in the *Analects* of Confucius, see Erin M. Cline, "Two

Senses of Justice: Confucianism, Rawls, and Comparative Political Philosophy," *Dao: A Journal of Comparative Philosophy* 6, no. 4 (winter 2007): 361–81.

16. If one conceives of our moral nature in terms of general ethical abilities and qualities, together with things like a capacity for moral improvement, one can begin to craft a picture of human beings as fundamentally worthy of special moral status and consideration. Such a view could be sketched in ways that avoid filling in the details of a substantive ethical view about the good and so might well function as the basis for a conception of human rights.

17. For a revealing comparative discussion of Mencius's views on war, see Daniel A. Bell, *Beyond Liberal Democracy* (Princeton, N.J.: Princeton University Press, 2006), 23–51. See also Julia Ching, "Confucianism and WMD," in *Ethics and Weapons of Mass Destruction: Religious and Secular Perspectives*, ed. Sohail H. Hashmi and Steven P. Lee, 246–69 (Cambridge: Cambridge University Press, 2004); and Philip J. Ivanhoe, "Heaven's Mandate and the Concept of War," in ibid., 270–76.

18. For a defense of the religious quality of the philosophies of Confucius and Mencius, see Philip J. Ivanhoe, "Heaven as a Source for Ethical Warrant in Early Confucianism," *Dao: A Journal of Comparative Philosophy* 6, no. 3 (2007): 211–20. Xunzi, the third major Confucian of the pre-Qin period, is an exception to the claims defended in this essay.

19. Munro argues that the religious elements of Mencius's philosophy should be eliminated in order to make it more palatable for the twenty-first century. ("Mencius and an Ethics of the New Century," in *Mencius: Contexts and Interpretations*, 305–15, reprinted in *Chinese Ethics for the New Century*, 61–70). I have argued for the value of the more religious dimensions of Mencius's thought in a short review of *Mencius: Contexts and Interpretations*, which appeared in the *Journal of Chinese Religions* 31 (2003): 215–16.

20. For a study that explores these stories as well as a wide range of accounts about women's virtue in traditional China, see Lisa A. Raphals, *Sharing the Light: Representations of Women and Virtue in Early China* (Albany: SUNY Press, 1998).

21. For this idea especially in regard to elite members of society, see Wm. Theodore de Bary, *Nobility and Civility: Asian Ideals of Leadership and the Common Good* (Cambridge, Mass.: Harvard University Press, 2004).

MENCIUS

BOOK IA

1] Mencius met with King Hui of Liang.[1]

The king said, "Venerable sir, you have not considered a thousand *li*[2] too far to come. Surely you have some means to profit our state?"

Mencius replied: "Why must the king speak of profit? I have only [teachings concerning] humaneness and rightness. If the king says, 'How can I profit my state?' the officers will say, 'How can I profit my house?' and the gentlemen and the common people will say, 'How can I profit myself?' Those above and those below will compete with one another for profit, and the state will be imperiled. One who murders the ruler over a state of ten thousand chariots surely will be from a house of a thousand chariots; one who murders the ruler over a state of a thousand chariots surely will be from a house of a hundred chariots.[3] A share of a thousand in ten thousand or a hundred in a thousand is hardly negligible; yet, when rightness is subordinated to profit the urge to lay claim to more becomes irresistible. It has never happened that one given to humaneness abandons his parents, nor that one given to rightness subordinates the interests of his lord. Let the king speak only of humaneness and rightness. What need has he to speak of profit?"

2] Mencius went to see King Hui of Liang. As he stood overlooking a pond, watching the geese and the deer, the king asked, "Do the virtuous also enjoy such things?"

1. King Hui of Liang was known during his lifetime as Marquis Ying of Wei, or, after moving his capital to Daliang, in 361, as Marquis Ying of Liang. Having ruled from 370 to 319 B.C.E., he became known posthumously as King Hui of Liang.

2. A *li* 里 is a unit of linear measure equal to around a third of a mile.

3. The chariot was used for military purposes and therefore the importance of a state was measured in terms of the number of chariots it possessed and could field.

Mencius replied, "Only the virtuous [truly] are able to enjoy these things. Those who are not virtuous, although they might have such things, cannot [truly] enjoy them.[4] The ode says,

> He began by measuring the spirit tower,
> He measured it and planned it.
> The common people worked on it,
> Finishing before a day was out.
> In beginning to measure he urged against haste,
> Yet the people came as if they were his children.
> The king was in the spirit park,
> The doe lying down,
> The doe glistening,
> The white bird glittering.
> The king was by his spirit pond,
> How full it was with dancing fish![5]

"King Wen used the strength of the people to build his tower and his pond, and the people found their delight and their joy in it. They called his tower 'the spirit tower' and his pond 'the spirit pond' and found joy in his having deer, and birds, and turtles. The ancients shared their joys with the people and it was this that enabled them to feel joy.

" 'The Declaration of Tang' says,

> O sun, when will you perish?
> We will die along with you.[6]

---

4. As Mencius will go on to argue, only a virtuous person can enjoy such things with others and thereby enjoy them fully. He also invokes the idea, seen in texts like the *Xunzi*, that a ruler who does not share his joy with his people cannot remain secure in his enjoyment of such pleasures.

5. Ode 242. See James Legge, trans., *The Chinese Classics*, 5 vols. (Hong Kong: University of Hong Kong Press, 1970), 4:456–57. The ode refers, as Legge puts it, to "the joy of the people in the growing opulence and dignity of King Wen."

6. From the *Classic of Documents*, in Legge, *Chinese Classics*, 3:175. The passage refers to the people's desire for the death of Jie, known as the "bad last ruler" of the Xia dynasty. The apparent meaning is that the people were so anxious to see Jie's death that they were willing to die themselves if this would ensure his death as well.

"If the people wished to die along with him, although he had a tower and pond, how could he enjoy them alone?"

[3] King Hui of Liang said, "I, this solitary man,[7] devotes his entire mind to the state. When the year is bad within the river, I transfer people to the east of the river and transfer grain to the area within the river. When the year is bad to the east of the river, again, I act accordingly. Look into the governments of neighboring states: there is no one as mindful as I, and yet people in the neighboring states do not decrease, nor do my people increase. Why should this be?"

Mencius said, "The king is fond of war; so please allow an analogy that derives from war. Drums rumbling, the soldiers having crossed weapons, some then flee, abandoning their armor and trailing their weapons behind them. Some stop after a hundred paces and some after fifty paces. How would it be if those who ran only fifty paces were to laugh at those who ran a hundred paces?"

The king said, "That would not do. It was only that they did not run a hundred paces, that is all. But they ran just the same."

Mencius said, "If the king understands this, there is no reason to expect the people to be more numerous than they are in neighboring states. If the agricultural seasons are not interfered with, there will be more grain than can be eaten. If close-meshed nets are not allowed in the pools and ponds, there will be more fish and turtles than can be eaten. And if axes are allowed in the mountains and forests only in the appropriate seasons, there will be more timber than can be used. When grain, fish, and turtles are more than can be eaten, and timber is more than can be used, this will mean that the people can nourish their lives, bury their dead, and be without rancor. Making it possible for them to nourish their lives, bury their dead, and be without rancor is the beginning of kingly government.

"Let mulberry trees be planted around households of five *mu*,[8] and people of fifty will be able to be clothed in silk. In the raising of chickens,

---

7. The Chinese term *gua ren* 寡人 (literally, lonely or friendless person) was one used by rulers to speak of themselves. It implies a sense (or pretense) of self-depreciation. Hereafter, it will be translated simply as "I."

8. A *mu* 畝 is a measure of area; 6.6 *mu* equal 1 acre.

pigs, dogs, and swine, do not neglect the appropriate breeding times, and people of seventy will be able to eat meat. With fields of a hundred *mu* do not interfere with the appropriate seasons of cultivation, and families with several mouths to feed will be able to avoid hunger. Attend carefully to the education provided in the schools,[9] which should include instruction in the duty of filial and fraternal devotion, and gray-haired people will not be seen carrying burdens on the roads. The ruler of a state in which people of seventy wear silk and eat meat and where the black-haired people are neither hungry nor cold has never failed to become a true king.[10]

"The king's dogs and pigs eat food intended for human beings and he does not know enough to prohibit this. On the roads there are people dying of starvation, and he does not know enough to distribute food. People die, and he says, 'It was not I; it was the year.' How is this different from killing a person by stabbing him and then saying, 'It was not I; it was the weapon'? When the king ceases to place the blame on the year, then the people of the world will come to him."

[1A4] King Hui of Liang said, "I would like a quiet moment in which to receive your instruction."

Mencius replied, saying, "Is there any difference between killing a man with a stick or killing him with a blade?"

He said, "There is no difference."

"And if it were done with a blade or through government, would there be any difference?"

He said, "There is no difference."

Mencius said, "In your kitchen, there is fat meat, and in your stables fat horses. Yet the people have a hungry look, and out beyond, in the more wild regions, lie the bodies of those who have died of starvation. This is to lead animals to devour people.[11] Now, animals devour

9. Mencius here mentions two kinds of schools, the *xiang* 庠 and the *xu* 序. In 3A3, he refers to these and several more, explaining that *xiang* was a Zhou term, while *xu* was a term used in the Yin or Shang dynasty.

10. That is to say, one who attracts loyal subjects to him and thereby unifies the empire.

11. In 3B9, the preceding three sentences are attributed to Gongming Yi, identified by Zheng Xuan in his commentary on the "Jiyi" chapter of the *Book of Rites* (*Liji* 禮記) as a disciple of Zengzi.

one another, and people hate this about them. If one governs as father and mother of the people and yet is not deterred from leading animals to devour people, in what sense is he father and mother of the people? Confucius said, 'The one who first made grave figures—was he not without posterity?'[12] This was because he made human images for such a use. How then should it be with one who causes his people to die of starvation?"

5] King Hui of Liang said, "Under Heaven there was no state stronger than Jin,[13] as you, venerable sir, are aware. But when it came to my reign, Jin was defeated by Qi in the east, and my oldest son died there. In the west seven hundred *li* were lost to Qin, while in the south we were humiliated by Chu.[14] Having incurred such shame, I wish, for the sake of the departed, to expunge it. How may this be done?"

Mencius replied, "With a territory of no more than one hundred *li*, one can become a true king. If the king bestows humane government on the people, reduces punishments, and lightens taxes, causing the plowing to be deep and the weeding thorough, the strong will be able to use their leisure time to cultivate filiality and brotherliness. Within the home they will serve their fathers and brothers; outside they will serve their elders and superiors. They can then be made to take up sticks and overcome the strong armor and the sharp weapons of Qin and Chu.

"Those other rulers lay claim to the time of their people, so that they are unable to plow or to weed and thus to nourish their parents. Their parents then suffer from cold and hunger; older and younger brothers are parted; wives and children are separated. These rulers bury their people and drown them. Were you to go and punish them, who would

12. These were wooden images in human form used in burials in the belief that they could perform service for the deceased. This, though, reinforces the deeply inhumane idea and encourages the practice of human sacrifices to the dead.

13. In the middle of the fifth century B.C.E., the state of Jin was divided up among the ruling families of Han, Zhao, and Wei and became known as the three Jin. King Hui is here referring to his state of Wei.

14. The chain of events referred to by King Hui began when Jin attacked Han and Han called for help from Qi.

oppose you?[15] Therefore, it may be said that the humane man has no enemy. May it please the king to have no doubt about this."[16]

[1A6] Mencius saw King Xiang of Liang.[17] On emerging he said to someone, "Seeing him from a distance, he does not appear to be a ruler of men; approaching him, one sees nothing imposing about him. He abruptly asked, 'How can the empire be settled?'

"I replied: 'It can be settled through unity.'

" 'Who is able to unite it?'

"I replied: 'One who is not fond of killing people can unite it.'

" 'Who can give it to him?'

"I replied: 'There is no one in the empire who will deny it to him. Does the king know the way of seedlings? If there is drought in the seventh or eighth month, the seedlings dry out. But when dense clouds gather in the sky and the rain falls in torrents the plants spring up and are revived. When this happens, who can stop them? Now, among the herders of men in the world there is none who is not fond of killing people. If there were one who was not fond of killing people, the people of the empire would crane their necks to look for him. If this were truly to happen, the people would return to him like water flowing downward, torrentially—who could stop them?' "

[1A7] King Xuan of Qi[18] asked, "Would it be possible to hear about the affairs of Duke Huan of Qi and Duke Wen of Jin?"[19]

---

15. The word translated "punish" here is *zheng* 征, which has the special connotation of a justified military campaign carried out by a legitimate authority. Compare 1B11, 7B2, and 7B4.

16. For Mencius's judgment of King Hui, see 7B1.

17. The successor to King Hui, he ruled from 318 to 296 B.C.E.

18. King Xuan ruled in the powerful state of Qi from 319 to 301 B.C.E.

19. Duke Huan of Qi (r. 685–643 B.C.E.), one of the most powerful feudal lords of the seventh century, was considered the first of the "Five Hegemons," and Duke Wen of Jin (r. 636–628 B.C.E.) was considered the second. Mencius's statement in the ensuing passage that he has "heard nothing about" these hegemons is not to be taken literally. The reputation of neither ruler was entirely negative, but Mencius is making the point here that he prefers to talk about true kings (*wang* 王) rather than lord-protectors or hegemons (*ba* 霸), whose claim to rule was believed by Confucians to be, morally speaking, more ambiguous.

Mencius replied, "The followers of Confucius did not speak of the affairs of Huan and Wen, and thus nothing about them has been transmitted to later generations. Not having heard, and having nothing to say on that matter, how would it be if I were to speak about being a true king?"

The king said, "What must one's Virtue be like in order to become a true king?"[20]

Mencius said, "One who protects the people becomes a true king, and no one is able to stop him."

"Could someone like me protect the people?"

"He could."

"How do you know that I could?"

"I have heard Hu He say that while the king was seated in the upper part of the hall someone led an ox past the hall below [in the courtyard]. On seeing this, the king asked where the ox was going and was told that it was being taken to serve as a blood sacrifice in the consecration of a bell. The king said, 'Spare it. I cannot bear its trembling, like one who, though blameless, is being led to the execution ground.' Asked whether in that case the consecration of the bell should be dispensed with, the king said, 'How can it be dispensed with? Substitute a sheep instead.' Did this actually happen?"

"It did."

Mencius said, "With such a mind[21] one has what it takes to become a true king. Though the people all thought it was because the king grudged the ox, I know it was surely because the king could not bear to see its suffering."

The king said, "That is so. The people must truly have thought this, but, although the state of Qi is small and narrow, how could I grudge a single ox? It was because I could not bear its trembling—like one who,

---

20. The word translated "Virtue" here is *de* 德. It connotes the moral quality of a person's character—good or bad. One with abundant, good Virtue enjoys a kind of moral charisma, which attracts and secures the support of others. For a study of this notion in early Chinese philosophy, see David S. Nivison, " 'Virtue' in Bronze and Bone" and "The Paradox of 'Virtue,' " both in *The Ways of Confucianism: Investigations in Chinese Philosophy*, ed. Bryan W. Van Norden, 17–43 (La Salle, Ill.: Open Court, 1996).

21. In speaking of "such a mind," Mencius is obviously referring not to the king's intellective or rational abilities but to his capacity for empathy.

though blameless, was being led to the execution ground—that I had a sheep substituted instead."

Mencius said, "The king should not think it strange that the people assumed that he grudged the ox. How could they know why he substituted the smaller creature for the larger one? If the king had been grieved over its being led, blameless, to the execution ground, then what was there to choose between an ox and a sheep?"

The king smiled and said, "What kind of mind was this, after all? It was not that I grudged the expense, yet I did exchange the ox for a sheep. No wonder the people said that I grudged it."

Mencius said, "There is no harm in this. This was after all the working of humaneness—a matter of having seen the ox but not the sheep. This is the way of the noble person in regard to animals: if he sees them alive, then he cannot bear to see them die, and if he hears their cries, then he cannot bear to eat their flesh. And so the noble person stays far away from the kitchen."

The king was pleased and said, "When the ode says, 'What other people have in their minds, I measure by reflection,'[22] it is speaking about someone like you. When I tried reflecting, going back and seeking my motive, I was unable to grasp my own mind. Yet when you spoke of it, my mind experienced a kind of stirring. How is it that this mind of mine accords with that of a true king?"

Mencius replied, "Suppose someone were to report to the king, saying, 'My strength, while sufficient to lift a hundred *jun*, is not sufficient to lift a feather.[23] My sight, while sufficient to scrutinize the tip of an autumn hair, is not sufficient to see a cartload of firewood.' Would the king accept this?"

"No," he said.

"How do these examples differ from the case of kindness sufficient to extend to animals yet without its benefits reaching the people? Not lifting a feather is the result of not exerting one's strength to do so; not seeing a cartload of firewood is the result of not employing his eyesight on it. That the people are not protected is because one does not exercise

---

22 Ode 198. Translation adapted from Legge, *Chinese Classics*, 4:342.

23. A *jun* 鈞 was a traditional measure of weight, around 30 catties, or 40 pounds.

kindness toward them. Therefore, that the king is not a true king is because he does not do it; it is not because he is unable to do it."

The king asked, "How can one distinguish between 'not doing something' and 'not being able to do it'?"[24]

Mencius said, "If it were a matter of taking Mount Tai under one's arm and jumping over the North Sea with it, and one were to tell people, 'I am unable to do it,' this would truly be a case of being unable to do it. If it is a matter of bowing respectfully to an elder, and one tells people, 'I am unable to do it,' this is a case of not doing it rather than a case of being unable to do it.[25] And so the king's failure to be a true king is not in the category of taking Mount Tai under one's arm and jumping over the North Sea with it; his failure to be a true king is in the category of not bowing respectfully to an elder. By treating the elders in one's own family as elders should be treated and extending this to the elders of other families, and by treating the young of one's own family as the young ought to be treated and extending this to the young of other people's families, the empire can be turned around on the palm of one's hand.[26] The ode says,

He set an example for his wife;
It extended to his brothers,
And from there to the family of the state.[27]

"This ode simply speaks of taking this mind and extending it to others. Thus, if one extends his kindness it will be enough to protect

24. For a discussion of the issue raised in this and other passages in *Mencius* concerning the difference between not doing something and not being able to do it, see David S. Nivison, "Mengzi: Just Not Doing It," in *Essays on the Moral Philosophy of Mengzi*, ed. Xiusheng Liu and Philip J. Ivanhoe, 132–42 (Indianapolis: Hackett, 2002).

25. The interpretation of this line is influenced by the very helpful comments of Yang Bojun (Yang Bojun, 楊伯峻, *Mengzi yizhu* 孟子譯注 [Beijing: Zhonghua shuju, 1960], 24, n. 24).

26. What Mencius means by "extension" is a matter that has generated considerable scholarly debate. For a review of this literature, see Philip J. Ivanhoe, "Confucian Self-Cultivation and Mengzi's Notion of Extension," in *Essays on the Moral Philosophy of Mengzi*, 221–41.

27. Ode 240 is a poem about the morally influential mother of King Wen. See Legge, *Chinese Classics*, 4:446–48.

all within the four seas, whereas if one fails to extend it, he will have no way to protect his wife and children.[28] The reason the ancients so greatly surpassed most people was nothing other than this: they were good at extending what they did. Now, your kindness is sufficient to extend to the animals but the benefits do not reach the people. Why do you make an exception in the case [of the people]?

"It is by weighing that we know which things are light and which are heavy, and by measuring that we know which are long and which are short. This is true of all things, and especially so with regard to the mind. May it please the king to measure his mind. When the king raises arms, endangers his subjects, and excites the enmity of the other feudal lords—does this perhaps bring pleasure to his mind?"

The king replied, "No. How could I take pleasure from this? It is just that I seek to realize what I greatly desire."

"May I hear about what it is that the king greatly desires?"

The king smiled and did not speak.

Mencius said, "Is it that the king does not have enough rich and sweet foods to satisfy his mouth? Or enough light and warm clothing for his body? Or enough beautiful colors for his eyes to gaze upon, or enough sounds for his ears to listen to? Is it that he does not have servants enough to come before him and receive orders? The king's ministers are sufficient to provide for all of this. How could the king's desire be for any of these things?"

He said, "No, it is none of these."

Mencius said, "Then what the king greatly desires can be known. His desire is to expand his territory, to bring Qin and Chu into his court, to rule the Central Kingdom, and to pacify the four Yi.[29] But to pursue such a desire by acting in the way you do is like climbing a tree in search of a fish."

The king said, "Is it as bad as *that*?"

"It is even *worse*. When one climbs a tree in search of a fish, though one gets no fish, no disaster will ensue. But if one acts in the way you do in pursuit of what you desire, and devotes the full strength of his mind to such endeavor, disaster is bound to ensue."

28. Mencius makes a similar claim in 2A6.
29. The four Yi were non-Chinese peoples.

"May I hear about this?"

"If the people of Zou were to go to war with the people of Chu, who, in the king's opinion, would win?"

"The people of Chu would win."

"Thus the small definitely cannot contend with the large, the few definitely cannot contend with the many, and the weak definitely cannot contend with the strong. Within the seas, there are nine territories of a thousand leagues square, and Qi is only one of them. What difference is there between one part attacking the other eight and Zou contending with Chu? Why not rather return to the root of the matter? If the king were to institute a government that dispensed humaneness, he would make all the officers in the world wish to stand in his court, all the tillers wish to till his fields, all the merchants wish to entrust their goods to his marketplaces, and all travelers wish to journey upon his roads. All those in the world who have grievances to express against their rulers would wish to lay their complaints before him. If you could bring this to pass, who could stop you from becoming a true king?

The king said, "I am unintelligent and incapable of following this advice. I should like you to assist my will and be clear in giving me instruction, so that, while not clever, I may endeavor to carry it out."

"It is only a gentleman who will be able to have a constant mind despite being without a constant means of livelihood. The people, lacking a constant means of livelihood, will lack constant minds, and when they lack constant minds there is no dissoluteness, depravity, deviance, or excess to which they will not succumb. If, once they have sunk into crime, one responds by subjecting them to punishment—this is to entrap the people. With a person of humanity in a position of authority, how could the entrapment of the people be allowed to occur?[30] Therefore, an enlightened ruler will regulate the people's livelihood so as to ensure that, above, they have enough to serve their parents and, below, they have enough to support their wives and children. In years of prosperity they always have enough to eat; in years of dearth they are able to escape starvation. Only then does he urge the people toward goodness; accordingly, they find it easy to comply.

---

30. Mencius is recorded, in 3A3, as saying the same thing, in almost exactly the same words, to Duke Wen of Teng.

"At present, the regulation of the people's livelihood is such that, above, they do not have enough to serve their parents and, below, they do not have enough to support wives and children. Even in years of prosperity their lives are bitter, while in years of dearth they are unable to escape starvation. Under these circumstances they only try to save themselves from death, fearful that they will not succeed. How could they spare the time for the practice of rites and rightness?

"If the king wishes to put this into practice, he should return to the root of the matter.[31] Let mulberry trees be planted around households of five *mu*, and people of fifty will be able to be clothed in silk. In the raising of chickens, pigs, dogs, and swine, do not neglect the appropriate breeding times, and people of seventy will be able to eat meat. With fields of a hundred *mu*, do not interfere with the appropriate seasons of cultivation, and families with eight mouths to feed will be able to avoid hunger. Attend carefully to the education provided in the schools, which should include instruction in the duty of filial and fraternal devotion, and gray-haired people will not be seen carrying burdens on the roads. The ruler of a state in which people of seventy wear silk and eat meat and where the black-haired people are neither hungry nor cold has never failed to become a true king.

31. What Mencius describes here as returning to "the root of the matter," or to what is fundamental, repeats almost exactly what he said, in 1A3, to King Hui of Liang.

BOOK IB

1] On seeing Mencius, Zhuang Bao said, "When I met with the king he spoke to me of his enjoyment of music. I did not know how to respond."

Then he added, "What do you think about the enjoyment of music?"

Mencius replied, "If the king truly enjoyed music, the state of Qi would be doing quite well."

Another day, when Mencius went to see the king, he said, "Is it true that Your Majesty told Master Zhuang you enjoy music?"

Flushing with embarrassment, the king said, "Incapable of enjoying the music of the former kings, I only enjoy the music popular in the world today, nothing more."

Mencius said, "If you truly enjoyed music, the state of Qi would be doing quite well, for the music of today derives from the music of antiquity."

The king said, "Would you explain to me what you mean by that?"

Mencius said, "Which is more pleasurable—enjoying music by oneself or enjoying it in the company of others?"

"Enjoying it with others."

"Which is more pleasurable—enjoying it in the company of a few or enjoying it in the company of many?"

"Enjoying it with many."

"With your permission, I would like to speak to you about music. Now suppose the king is making music here. Hearing the echoes of the king's bells and drums and the sounds of his pipes and flutes, the people, with aching heads and furrowed brows, all ask one another, 'Why should our king's fondness for music make life so hard for us? Fathers and sons cannot see one another; older and younger brothers, wives and children are separated and scattered.' Now suppose the king is going hunting. Hearing the sounds of the king's chariots and horses and seeing the beauty of the plumage and banners, the people, with aching heads and furrowed brows, all ask one another, 'Why should our king's fondness for hunting make life so hard for us? Fathers and sons cannot see one another; older and younger brothers, wives and children are separated and scattered.' This is solely because he does not share his enjoyment with the people.

"Now suppose the king is making music here. Hearing the echoes of the king's bells and drums and the sounds of his pipes and flutes, the people, joyfully and with delighted countenances, all tell one another, 'Our king must be quite free of illness, for if he were ill, how would he be able to make music?' Now suppose the king is going hunting here. Hearing the sounds of the king's carriages and horses and seeing the beauty of the plumage and banners, the people, joyfully and with delighted countenances, all tell one another, 'Our king must be quite free of illness, for if he were ill, how would he be able to go hunting?' This is solely because he shares his enjoyment with the people. Now, if Your Majesty simply will share your enjoyment with the people, you shall be a true king."

[1B2] King Xuan of Qi asked, "Is it true that King Wen's park was seventy *li* square?"

Mencius replied, "It is so stated in the records."

He asked, "Was it as large as that?"

"The people still considered it small."

"My park is forty *li* square, yet the people consider it large. Why should this be?"

"The seventy-*li*-square park of King Wen was frequented by the gatherers of grass and rushes and by the hunters of pheasants and rabbits. He shared it with the people. It is only natural that they should have considered it small, is it not? When I first arrived at the borders of your state, I inquired, before daring to enter, about its greatest prohibitions. I was told that within the passes there is a park of forty *li* square where the crime of killing a deer is considered equivalent to the crime of killing a human being. Since this forty *li* square is a trap in the middle of the state, it is only natural that the people consider it large, is it not?"

3] King Xuan of Qi asked, "Is there a way of conducting relations with neighboring states?"

Mencius replied, "There is. But only one who is humane is able to serve a small state with a large one, as was the case when Tang served Ge and King Wen served the Kun tribes.[1] Only the wise are able to serve a large state with a small one, as was the case when Tai Wang served the Xunyu[2] and Goujian served Wu.[3] One who with a large state serves a small one delights in Heaven, while one who with a small state serves a large one is in awe of Heaven. Through delighting in Heaven one preserves all-under-Heaven, and through being in awe of Heaven one preserves his state. The ode says,

Being in awe of the majesty of Heaven,
I thus preserve it."[4]

The king said, "How great are these words! But I have a failing. I am fond of valor."

Mencius replied, "Let the king not be fond of *small* valor. One who grasps his sword, stares menacingly, and says, 'How dare he confront

1. For an account of the churlish and duplicitous behavior of the ruler of Ge and the humane response of the future King Tang of Shang to this behavior, see 3B5. King Wen of Zhou is supposed to have served the Kun (or Hun) tribes of the West, though exactly how he did so is unspecified.

2. Old Duke Danfu (Gugong Danfu), who became known as King Tai, was the grand-father of King Wen of Zhou. The duke reappears in 1B5, and Mencius's description of the Old Duke's response to an invasion of the territory of Bin by the Xunyu (or Di) tribes is found in 1B15.

3. According to the account in the "Memoir of Wu Zi Xu," in book 66 of *The Grand Scribe's Records*, the state of Yue defeated Wu in a battle in 496 B.C.E. in which the king of Wu, Holu, died. In 494, Holu's heir, Fuchai, went to war with Yue to avenge the death of his father. Yue was defeated. Moreover, rather than prolonging the conflict with Wu, the ruler of Yue, Goujian, was deferential toward Fuchai, presenting gifts to Wu's grand steward and offering up his state as slaves to Wu. Fuchai, against the advice of his adviser, Wu Zi Xu, accepted the offer. Some years later, while Fuchai's attention was directed elsewhere, Wu was attacked by Yue and suffered a crushing defeat. See Sima Qian, *The Grand Scribe's Records*, ed. William H. Nienhauser (Bloomington: Indiana University Press, 1994), 7:55–59.

4. Ode 272. Commentators differ over whether *bao zhi* 保之, the final two characters of the ode, should be interpreted as referring to the Mandate of Heaven or the favor of King Wen and Heaven. See Legge, *Chinese Classics*, 4:575–76.

me!' is displaying the valor of an ordinary man who is able to be the adversary of just one person. Let the king be greater than that.

"The ode says,

> The king, his anger blazing,
> Led forth and ordered his troops
> To repel the march on Ju,
> To reclaim the blessings of Zhou,
> To respond to all-under-Heaven.[5]

This was the valor of King Wen. In one burst of anger King Wen brought peace to all the people in the world. It says in the *Classic of Documents*:

> Heaven, in sending down the people,
> Made a ruler for them, made them a teacher,
> Saying just that he should help the Lord-on-High,
> Bestowing grace throughout the four quarters.
> I alone am here for whoever has done wrong
> And for whoever has done no wrong. How dare there
> Be under Heaven anyone with a will to transgress?[6]

There was one man who was enacting evil in the world, and King Wu was ashamed of this. This was the valor of King Wu. So King Wu, too, in one burst of anger, brought peace to all the people in the world. Now Your Majesty should also, in one burst of anger, bring peace to all the people in the world. The people are only afraid that you are *not* fond of valor."

[1B4] King Xuan of Qi received Mencius in the Snow Palace. The king asked, "Do such pleasures belong also to the worthy?"

Mencius replied, "They do. And yet if the people cannot have such pleasures, they blame their superiors. For them to blame their superi-

---

5. Ode 241 (ibid., 4:448–55).
6. See the "Great Declaration" (Taishi) chapter of the *Classic of Documents*, in ibid., 3:286.

ors because they do not have them is wrong, yet to be in a position of authority over the people and not to share one's pleasures with them is also wrong. When one takes pleasure in the people's pleasures, the people will also take pleasure in one's pleasures, and when one sorrows over the people's sorrows, they will also sorrow over one's sorrows. One who delights in what the world delights in and sorrows over what the world sorrows over—such a one never has failed to become a true king.

"Once Duke Jing of Qi[7] inquired of Minister Yan,[8] saying, 'I should like to go on a tour of inspection to Zhuanfu and Chaowu and then to proceed south, following the coast, to Langye. What must I do so that my tour can be compared to those of the former kings?'

"Minister Yan replied, 'An excellent question! The Son of Heaven's visits to the lords were called tours of inspection [*xun shou* 巡狩]. *Xun shou* means that he inspected the territory within his care [*xun suo shou* 巡所守].[9] The lords' visits to the Son of Heaven were called reports on responsibilities [*shu zhi* 述職]. *Shu zhi* means that they reported [*shu*] on the fulfillment of their responsibilities [*zhi*]. Both these excursions had their purpose. In spring they observed the plowing and corrected any deficiencies; in autumn they observed the harvesting and repaired any shortages.[10] In the Xia there was a saying,

> If our king does not journey,
> In whom can we find rest?
> If our king does not visit,
> From whom can we get help?
> Each journey, each visit,[11]
> Sets a standard for the lords.'

7. Duke Jing was a near contemporary of Confucius and the ruler of Qi in the closing years of the Spring and Autumn period.

8. Yan Ping, or Master Yan, was the chief minister of Qi during the reign of Duke Jing and was considered a particularly worthy man. In the *Analects* 5:16 Confucius is quoted as praising him for being respectful and adept at human relations.

9. This definition of a royal "tour of inspection" depends on the substitution of the character *shou*, meaning "to guard" or "to protect," for one with the same pronunciation that means "a tour of inspection."

10. There is a close resemblance between this account of royal visits to the lords and the lords' visits to the court of the Son of Heaven and one in 6B7.

11. Apparently referring to the spring and autumn inspections.

"It is no longer thus. An army on the march is provisioned, but there is no food for the hungry or rest for the weary. Eyes averted, complaining to one another, the people turn to evil. The mandate is violated, the people are oppressed; food and drink are wasted like water washing away. This waste, dissolution, depravity, and debauchery become a cause of sorrow for the lords.

"Following a downward course and forgetting to return is called wasting oneself; following an upward course and forgetting to return is called dissolution; to pursue animals insatiably is called depravity; to delight in drink without restraint is called debauchery.

"The former kings did not have pleasures that left them wasted or dissolute or travels that led them into depravity or debauchery. It is for you to set your own course.

"Duke Jing was pleased. He issued a proclamation throughout the state and went to live in a hut on the outskirts of the capital.[12] From that time on he opened his granaries to the needy. Summoning the music master, he said, 'Compose me songs suitable to express the sharing of pleasures between a ruler and his ministers.' What he made was the *zhi shao* [徵招] and the *jue shao* [角招],[13] the words to which say,

> What wrong is there in restraining one's lord?
> To restrain one's lord is to love him."[14]

[1B5] King Xuan of Qi asked, "Everyone tells me to demolish the Hall of Light. Should I demolish it or should I not?"

Mencius replied, "The Hall of Light is a hall of kings. If the king wishes to practice true kingly government, he should not demolish it."

---

12. He engaged in ritual preparation for his journey.

13. The musical scale was pentatonic, and, according to Zhu Xi, the third note was *jue* and the fourth was *zhi*, though he does not explain how the use of these two notes produced the music master's song; *shao* refers to the music of the sage-king Shun.

14. According to Zhu Xi, the most worthy minister is one who recognizes the need to help the ruler to control his desires. The translation of this passage is very tentative. Some commentators and translators have taken the view that the sentences that begin with "An army on the march is provisioned . . . " and continue to the end of the paragraph represent another quotation (comparable to the "Xia saying" that precedes them) and that the following paragraph (beginning, "Following a downward course . . . ") represents a commentary on or exegesis of the quotation. This interpretation is plausible but difficult to prove.

The king said, "May I hear about true kingly government?"

Mencius said, "In antiquity, when King Wen governed Qi,[15] tillers of the fields were taxed one part in nine and descendants of officers received emoluments. There was inspection but no taxation at border stations and in marketplaces; there was no restriction on the use of ponds and weirs. The wives and children of offenders were not implicated in their guilt. Old men without wives are called widowers; old women without husbands are called widows; the elderly without children are called desolates; the young without parents are called orphans—these four, the most destitute and the voiceless among the people, King Wen made his first concern, displaying humaneness in his conduct of government. The ode says,

> Fortunate indeed are those who prosper,
> But pity those who are alone and desolate."[16]

The king said, "What excellent words!"

Mencius said, "If the king finds them excellent, why does he not practice them?"

The king said, "I have a failing—I am fond of wealth."

Mencius replied, "In antiquity Gong Liu was fond of wealth. The ode says,

> Gathered up and storing,
> Bundling provisions in sacks and bags,
> He thought of bringing the people together,
> And bringing glory to the state.
> Bows and arrows were displayed,
> And shields, spears, and battle-axes,
> Only then did the march begin.[17]

Therefore, those who stayed at home had well-stocked granaries, and those on the march had well-prepared provisions: only then could the

---

15. Not King Xuan's state, but a Zhou territory in the western part of modern Shensi.
16. Ode 192 (Legge, *Chinese Classics*, 4:314–20).
17. Ode 250 (ibid., 4:483–89).

march begin. If the king shares his fondness of wealth with the people, how could this interfere with becoming a true king?"

The king said, "I have a failing—I am fond of women."[18]

"In antiquity King Tai was fond of women, and he loved his concubines. The ode says,

Old Duke Danfu[19] came in the morning,
Riding his horse by the western bank,
Reaching the foot of Mount Qi,
He brought the lady of Jiang along with him,
And there, together, they selected the site.

At that time, within the confines of home there were no dissatisfied women, and outside the home there were no unattached men. If the king shares his fondness of women with the people, how could this interfere with becoming a true king?"

[1B6] Mencius said to King Xuan of Qi, "Suppose that one of the king's subjects entrusted his wife and children to his friend and journeyed to Chu. On returning he found that the friend had subjected his wife and children to cold and hunger. What should he do?"

The king said, "Renounce him."

"Suppose the chief criminal judge could not control the officers. What should he do?"

The king said, "Get rid of him."

"Suppose that within the four borders of the state there is no proper government—then what?"

The king looked left and right and spoke of other things.

[1B7] Mencius went to see King Xuan of Qi. He said, "When we speak of an ancient state we do not mean that it has tall trees in it but that it has ministers from families that have served on a hereditary basis. The

---

18. *Se* 色, here translated "fond of women," has a range of meanings, including color, sensual beauty, and sexuality.

19. Old Duke Danfu was a descendant of Duke Liu; see note 2.

king no longer has ministers who are related to him. Those whom you advanced yesterday are, without your knowing it, gone today."

The king said, "How could I have known that they lacked ability and so have avoided employing them?"

"The ruler of a state employs men on the basis of their worthiness only when he must. Since this involves advancing those from lowly backgrounds over those from noble backgrounds and those who are remote from him over his relatives, must he not be cautious?

"When those on the left and right all say that someone is worthy, one should not yet believe it. When the great officers all say he is worthy, one should not yet believe it. When all the people in the state say that he is worthy, then one should investigate, and if one finds that he is worthy, only then should one employ him. When those on the left and right all say he is not acceptable, one should not yet believe it. When the great officers all say that he is not acceptable, one should not yet believe it. When all the people of the state say that he is not acceptable, one should investigate, and if one finds that he is not acceptable, only then should one send him away. When those on the left and the right say, 'He should be put to death,' one should not yet accept it. When the great officers all say, 'He should be put to death,' one should not yet accept it. When all the people of the state say, 'He should be put to death,' one should investigate, and if one finds that he should be put to death, only then should one put him to death. Thus we have the saying, 'The people of the state put him to death.' By acting thus one may be able to become the father and mother of the people."

B8] King Xuan of Qi asked, "Is it true that Tang banished Jie and King Wu assaulted *Zhou*?" [20]

Mencius replied, "It is so stated in the records."[21]

20. According to tradition, Tang, as the first ruler of the Shang dynasty, was responsible for ousting the depraved Jie, the last ruler of the Xia dynasty. King Wu, as one of the founders of the Zhou dynasty, is credited with deposing the wicked tyrant *Zhou*, the last ruler of the Shang. (The character for his name has the same sound as the character for the Zhou dynasty, and so I use italic letters to avoid confusion.)

21. Tang's ousting of Jie is recorded in "The Announcement of Zhong-hui" and "The Announcement of Tang," and King Wu's removal of *Zhou* in "The Great Declaration" and "The Successful Completion of the War," all in the *Classic of Documents*.

"Then can a minister be allowed to slay his ruler?"

"One who offends against humaneness is called a brigand; one who offends against rightness is called an outlaw. Someone who is a brigand and an outlaw is called a mere fellow. I have heard of the punishment of the mere fellow *Zhou* but never of the slaying of a ruler."

[1B9] Mencius went to see King Xuan of Qi. He said, "If one is going to build a hall, one will surely ask the master carpenter to obtain large trees. When the master carpenter has obtained large trees, the king will be pleased and will find him equal to the task. If one of the carpenters cuts them and makes them too small, the king will be angry and consider that he is unequal to the task. A person spends his youth in learning, and in his maturity wants to implement what he has learned. What if the king were to say, 'For the time being, put aside what you have learned and follow me'? Now suppose Your Majesty has a piece of uncarved jade. Although it is worth ten thousand *yi*, you will surely have the jade carver cut and polish it.

"If, though, when it comes to governing the state, Your Majesty were to say, 'For the time being, put aside what you have learned and follow me,' in what way is this different from instructing the jade carver on how to cut and polish the jade?"

[1B10] The people of Qi attacked Yan and defeated it. King Xuan asked, "Some say I should take possession of it and others say I should not. For a state of ten thousand chariots to attack another state of ten thousand chariots and to capture it within fifty days[22] is something that surpasses human strength. If I do not take possession of it, there must surely be calamities sent down by Heaven. What do you think about taking it?"

Mencius replied, "If taking it will cause the people of Yan to be pleased, then take it. Among the men of antiquity there was one who did this: King Wu. If taking it will cause the people of Yan to be displeased, then do not take it. Among the men of antiquity there was one who did this: King Wen. If a state of ten thousand chariots attacks another state of ten thousand chariots, and the people come with bas-

22. Literally, five *xun* 旬, or ten-day weeks.

kets of food and pitchers of drink to welcome the king's army, can it be for any reason other than to avoid flood and fire? If the water then gets deeper and the fire hotter, they will surely turn again."

11]   After the people of Qi had attacked Yan and taken possession of it, the rulers of the other states were making plans to rescue Yan. King Xuan said, "Many of the lords are making plans to attack me. How shall I prepare for them?"

Mencius replied, "I have heard that there was one with seventy *li* who extended his government to the entire realm: this was Tang. I have not heard of one with a thousand *li* who feared others. It says in the *Classic of Documents*:

> When Tang undertook the work of punishment
> He began with Ge.[23] The whole world trusted him.
> When he pursued the work of punishment in the east,
> The Yi in the west felt aggrieved; when he pursued
> The work of punishment in the south, the Di in the
> North felt aggrieved, saying, 'Why does he leave us
> Until last?'[24]

"The people looked to him as to clouds and rainbows in a time of great drought. Those going to market had no need to stop; those tilling the fields were unimpeded. He punished the rulers but comforted the people. He was like timely rain descending; the people were greatly pleased. The *Classic of Documents* says,

> We await our ruler; when he comes we will be revived.[25]

"Now, Yan oppressed its people, and you went and punished its ruler. The people believed you were going to deliver them from out of the flood and fire and, bringing baskets of rice and pitchers of drink, they welcomed

---

23. This quotation, while not identical, is close to the language of "The Announcement of Zhong-hui" in the *Classic of Documents* (Legge, *Chinese Classics*, 3:180).

24. Again, though the wording is slightly different, this quotation is close to the language of "The Announcement of Zhong-hui" in the *Classic of Documents* (Legge, *Chinese Classics*, 3:180–81).

25. Once again, the language closely resembles that of "The Announcement of Zhong-hui" (Legge, *Chinese Classics*, 3:181).

your army. Then you slew their fathers and older brothers, bound their sons and younger brothers, destroyed their ancestral temple, and carried off their treasured vessels—how can this be condoned? Certainly the world fears the might of Qi. Now you have doubled your territory but have not practiced humane government; it is this that is setting the troops of the realm in motion. If you will immediately issue orders to return the captives and halt the removal of the treasured vessels, and if you consult with the people of Yan about withdrawing once a ruler has been installed for them, you may still be able to stop an attack."

[1B12] There was a clash between Zou and Lu. Duke Mu[26] asked: "Thirty-three of my officers died, and none of the people died with them. If I were to put them to death, I could not put to death so many. But if I do not put them to death, the fact remains that they watched with looks of hatred as their superiors died and did nothing to save them. What is to be done about this?"

Mencius replied, "In years of calamity and years of famine, the old and weak among your people who were left to tumble over into drains and ditches and the strong who were scattered in the four directions numbered in the thousands. Meanwhile, the lord's granaries were full and his treasuries overflowing, and not one of the officers informed him—so callous were those above, so cruel toward those below. Master Zeng said, 'Beware! Beware! What comes forth from you will return to you.' When now the people are at last able to pay back what they have received, the lord should not blame them. If the lord practices humane government, the people will feel affection for their superiors and will die for their officers."

[1B13] Duke Wen of Teng asked, "Teng is a small state that lies between Qi and Chu. Should it serve Qi, or should it serve Chu?"

Mencius replied, "This is not something that lies within my competence, but if you insist on counsel, there is one thing to be said. Dig deep moats and build high walls; defend them together with the people. If, even in the face of death, the people do not leave you, this will show that your actions were right."

26. Duke Mu was the ruler of Zou, Mencius's native state.

4] Duke Wen of Teng asked, "The people of Qi are on the point of fortifying Xie. I am deeply fearful. What is to be done about this?"

Mencius replied, "Formerly, when King Tai dwelled in Bin, the Di people invaded it, and he left and went to dwell at the foot of Mount Qi. It was not that he chose to do this; he had no alternative. If you do good there will surely be among your descendants one who is a true king. The noble person creates a legacy and hands down a beginning that may be carried on. When it comes to achieving success—that is determined by Heaven. What can you do about Qi? Devote all your strength to being good, that is all."

5] Duke Wen of Teng asked, "Teng is a small state. I exert all my effort to serve the great states but get nowhere. What is to be done about this?"

Mencius replied, "Formerly, when King Tai[27] dwelled in Bin, the Di people invaded it. He served them with skins and with textiles but got nowhere. He served them with dogs and horses but got nowhere. He served them with pearls and jade but got nowhere. So he gathered together the elders and announced to them, 'What the Di people want is my territory. I have heard that a ruler does not use that whereby he nourishes the people to injure the people. My children, why should you grieve about not having a ruler? I will leave this place.' He left Bin, crossed Mount Liang, built a town at the foot of Mount Qi, and dwelled there. The people of Bin said, 'He is a humane person. We must not lose him.' Those who followed after him were as numerous as people going to market.

"Some say, 'A state is passed down from generation to generation; it is not something a single person can dispose of as he pleases. Even in the face of death one should not leave it.'

"If it pleases Your Majesty, he should choose between these two courses."

6] Duke Ping of Lu[28] was about to go out when his favorite, one Zang Cang, inquired: "On other occasions when my lord has gone out he has informed his officers of his destination. Today, while the carriages

27. Old Duke Danfu, or King Tai, has already appeared in 1B3 and 1B5.
28. Ping was the Duke's posthumous name; during his lifetime he was called Shu and also Shi.

are already yoked, the officers do not yet know where he is going. I beg leave to ask."

The duke said, "To see Mencius."

"Why? Is the lord to demean himself by initiating a visit to a common man because he considers him to be worthy? Rites and rightness emanate from the worthy, but Mencius's second mourning surpassed his first.[29] The lord should not go to see him."

The duke said, "Very well."

Master Yuezhengzi[30] came in to see the duke and said, "Why have you not gone to see Meng Ke?"[31]

"Someone told me that Mencius's second mourning surpassed his first, and so I did not go to see him."

"Why? When you speak of 'surpassing' you must mean that on the former occasion he observed the rites befitting a man of service and on the latter occasion the rites appropriate to a great officer, that on the former occasion he employed three sacrificial vessels and on the latter occasion five sacrificial vessels."

"No, I was referring to the fineness of the inner and outer coffins, the grave clothes, and the coverings."

"This was not a matter of 'surpassing' but of the difference in his means."[32]

When Master Yuezheng saw Mencius he said, "I told my lord about you, and he was going to come to see you when one of his favorites, a certain Zang Cang, stopped him. And so he did not come after all."

Mencius said, "When one goes forward there is something that impels the action; when one stops, there is something that impedes it. Going forward and stopping are not within a person's capacity to control. My not meeting the lord of Lu was owing to Heaven. How could this son of the Zang family have been the cause of my not meeting him?"

---

29. The first mourning observed by Mencius was for his father, who died while Mencius was very young. The second was for his mother.

30. Yuezheng Ke was an official in the state of Lu and a disciple of Mencius's.

31. Referring to Mencius by his name rather than by the title Master Meng.

32. Mencius was more affluent at the time of his mother's death than he had been at the time of his father's death. For more on Mencius's views of the appropriate way of mourning the death of a parent and of conducting the burial rites, see 2B7.

BOOK 2A

[AI] Gongsun Chou asked, "If you, Master, were to hold high office in Qi, could you promise to replicate the achievements of a Guan Zhong or a Yanzi?"

Mencius said, "Truly, you are a man of Qi. You know only of Guan Zhong and Yanzi, nothing more.

"Someone asked Zeng Xi, 'As between you and Zilu, who is the more worthy?' Looking discomfited, Zeng Xi said, 'He was one for whom my father had profound respect.' 'As between you and Guan Zhong, who is the more worthy?' His countenance changing to an expression of displeasure, Zengzi said, 'How is it that you compare me with Guan Zhong? So completely did Guan Zhong hold the confidence of his ruler, so long was he occupied with affairs of state, and yet so unimpressive were his achievements—how is it that you compare me to him?'

'Mencius said, "Though Guan Zhong was not someone Zengzi would choose to be, is this nonetheless what you want for me?"

"Guan Zhong made his ruler a hegemon. Yanzi made his ruler illustrious. Are Guan Zhong and Yanzi still not worthy of being followed?"

"To make the ruler of Qi a true king would be like turning over one's hand."[1]

"If that is so, then my confusion is all that much greater. Even the Virtue of King Wen, who lived to be over one hundred years old, had not penetrated all-under-Heaven within his lifetime. King Wu and the Duke of Zhou followed him, and only then did King Wen's Virtuous influence pervade throughout the world. Now, when you say that to

---

1. That is, very easy.

become a true king is easy, does this mean that King Wen is not worthy of being followed?"

"How could King Wen be equaled? From Tang[2] down to Wuding there were six or seven worthy and sagely rulers. For a long time all-under-Heaven had belonged to Yin,[3] long enough that it was difficult to change. Wuding had the various lords coming to his court and possessed all-under-Heaven as if he were turning it around on his palm. The interlude between *Zhou* and Wuding was not long,[4] and the inherited customs of the old families and the legacy of good government still persisted. Then there were the Viscount of Wei, Wei Zhong, Prince Bigan, the Viscount of Ji, and Jiao Ge, all of them worthy men who, together, assisted *Zhou*, so that it was a long time before he lost it.[5] There was not a foot of ground that he did not possess nor was there a single person who was not his subject. King Wen, on the other hand, started with only a hundred *li* square—which is why it was difficult.

"The people of Qi have a saying: 'Though you are intelligent, it is better to take advantage of circumstances. Though you have a hoe, it is better to wait for the proper season.' In the present time, it would be easy.

"In the flourishing periods of the Xia, Yin, and Zhou, the domain did not exceed a thousand *li*, and Qi has this much land. The sound of cocks crowing and dogs barking extends to the four borders, so Qi has the people. No extension of the territory and no increase in population are necessary. If he will practice humane government, he will become a true king, and no one will be able to stand in his way. Moreover, there has never been a longer time since a true king appeared, never a time when the people's sufferings from tyrannical government have been so great. It is easy to provide food for the hungry, easy to provide drink for the thirsty. Confucius said, 'The transmission of Virtue is faster than the transmission of an order through the post.'

"At the present time, if humane government were established in a state of ten thousand chariots, the people would be as pleased as if they had been freed from hanging upside down. Thus one can with half the

---

2. Founder of the Shang dynasty.
3. Yin was another name for the Shang.
4. Something less than two hundred years.
5. That is, before he lost the rulership as the Shang was displaced by the Zhou.

effort of the ancients bring about twice their achievements—if only it is done now."

2] Gongsun Chou asked, "If you, Master, were appointed a high minister of Qi and were able to put the Way into practice, it would not be surprising if the ruler were to become a hegemon or even king. If this were to occur, would your mind be moved or not?"

Mencius said, "No, since the age of forty my mind has been unmoved."

"In that case you far surpass Meng Ben."

"That is not difficult. Gaozi attained an unmoved mind before I did."

"Is there a way to attain an unmoved mind?"

"There is. Bogong You's way of nourishing his valor was neither to shrink from blows nor to avert his gaze. He thought that merely to be jostled by someone was like being flogged in the marketplace. What he would not accept from a poor fellow clad in coarse clothing he would not accept from a lord with ten thousand chariots, and he would cut down the lord with ten thousand chariots as soon as he would the poor man, coarsely clad. He had no regard for any of the lords, and if an insult came his way, he would invariably return it.

"Meng Shishe's way of nourishing his valor is expressed in his saying, 'I regard defeat just as I do victory. To advance only after having assessed the strength of the enemy, to engage only after having calculated the prospects for victory—this is to be intimidated by the opposing force. How can I be certain of victory? I can only be fearless, that is all.'

"Meng Shishe resembled Zengzi, while Bogong You resembled Zixia. I do not know which kind of valor should be considered superior, but Meng Shishe kept hold of what is essential. Formerly, Zengzi said to Zixiang, 'Do you admire valor? I once heard this account of great valor from the Master:[6] "If, on looking inward, I find that I am not upright, I must be in fear of even a poor fellow in coarse clothing. If, on looking inward, I find that I am upright, I may proceed against thousands and tens of thousands."' So Meng Shishe's keeping hold of his physical

6. That is, Confucius.

energy [*qi* 氣] was, after all, not comparable to Zengzi's keeping hold of what is essential."

"May I venture to ask you, Master, about your unmoved mind compared to Gaozi's unmoved mind?"

"Gaozi said, 'What you do not get in words, do not seek in the mind; what you do not get in the mind, do not seek in the *qi*.'[7] It may be acceptable to say that what one does not get in the mind should not be sought in the *qi*. But it is unacceptable to say that what one does not get in words should not be sought in the mind. The will is the leader of the *qi*, and it is *qi* that fills the body. When the will goes forward, the *qi* follows it. Therefore I say, maintain the will and do no violence to the *qi*.'"

"Since you say, 'When the will goes forward, the *qi* follows it,' why is it that you also say, 'maintain the will and do no violence to the *qi*'?"

"If the will is unified, it moves the *qi*, whereas if the *qi* is unified, it moves the will. Now, when a person stumbles or runs, it is the *qi* that acts, but it also moves the mind."

"May I presume to ask you, Master, in what do you excel?"

"I understand words. I am good at nourishing my vast, flowing *qi*."

"May I presume to ask what is meant by 'vast, flowing *qi*'?"

"It is difficult to put into words. This *qi* is consummately great and consummately strong. If one nourishes it with uprightness and does not injure it, it will fill the space between Heaven and earth. This *qi* is the companion of rightness and the Way, in the absence of which, it starves. It is born from an accumulation of rightness rather than appropriated through an isolated display. If one's actions cause the mind to be disquieted, it starves. I therefore said that Gaozi did not understand rightness because he regarded it as external.

"Always be doing something, but without fixation, with a mind inclined neither to forget nor to help things grow. One should not be like

---

7. The meaning of Gaozi's statement has been subject to a variety of interpretations, one of which is that human moral standards derive from "words"—that is, from moral teachings, and not from one's own mind or psychophysical energy. Note that, in addition to the three terms used by Gaozi—words, mind, and *qi*—Mencius introduces the term "will." What is clear from Mencius's disagreement with Gaozi is that Mencius himself believed that words, the mind (or will), and physical energy were all closely interrelated.

the man of Song. There was a man of Song, who, worried that his seedlings were not growing, pulled them up. Having done so, he returned home wearily, telling people, 'I am tired today—I have been helping the seedlings to grow.' When his sons rushed out to have a look, they found all the seedlings were withered. There are few in the world who do not try to help the seedlings to grow. Those who believe there is no way to benefit them neglect the seedlings and do not weed them. Those bent on helping them to grow pull them up, which is not only of no benefit but, on the contrary, causes them injury."[8]

"What is meant by 'understanding words'?"

"From distorted words, one knows the obscuration; from licentious words, one knows the corruption; from deviant words, one knows the waywardness; from evasive words, one knows the desperation. What is born in the mind does damage to government, and what arises in government does damage to the conduct of affairs. If a sage were to arise again, he would certainly follow my words."

"Zai Wo and Zigong were good at speaking. Ran Niu, Min Zi, and Yan Yuan were good with words and with Virtuous action. Though Confucius brought together both of these, he said, 'I have no great facility with words.' Then are you, Master, already a sage?"

"What words are these? Formerly Zigong asked Confucius, 'Is the Master a sage?' Confucius said, 'A sage I cannot be. I am, in learning, indefatigable and, in teaching, untiring.' Zigong said, 'Your learning indefatigably—this is wisdom. Your teaching untiringly—this is humaneness. Being humane and being wise, the Master is indeed a sage.' Since Confucius would not assent to being regarded as a sage, what words are these?"

"I once heard that Zixia, Ziyou, and Zizhang each had one of the qualities of the sage, while Ran Niu, Min Zi, and Yan Yuan had all of the qualities, but in slighter degree. I venture to ask with which of these you are willing to be compared?"

"Let us have done with this discussion."

"What about Boyi and Yi Yin?"

---

8. David S. Nivison suggests that the language of this passage resonates with that in 7A3 ("On Translating Mencius," in *The Ways of Confucianism: Investigations in Chinese Philosophy*, ed. Bryan W. Van Norden [La Salle, Ill.: Open Court, 1996], 182).

"Our ways are different. Not to serve a ruler who was not his own, nor to lead a people not his own; to advance when there was order and to withdraw when there was disorder—this was Boyi. To serve any ruler, to lead any people; to advance when there was order, and likewise to advance when there was disorder—this was Yi Yin. To serve in office when it was proper to serve, to stop when it was proper to stop; to continue when it was proper to continue and to withdraw when it was proper to withdraw—this was Confucius. They were all sages of antiquity. I have not been able to do what they did, but the one I want to learn from is Confucius."

"Can Boyi and Yi Yin be compared to Confucius?"

"No. Since the beginning of human life, there has never been another Confucius."

"Then did they have anything in common with Confucius?"

"They did. If they had ruled over a hundred *li* of territory, they would all have been able to bring the various lords to their court and to possess all-under-Heaven. None would have performed one act that was not right or killed one innocent person in order to possess all-under-Heaven. These things they shared in common with Confucius."

"I venture to ask in what ways they differed from Confucius."

"Zai Wo, Zigong, and Yu Zuo were wise enough to know the sage. Though they had a low opinion of themselves, they would not have come to the point of flattering someone just because they liked him. Zai Wo said, 'As I see the Master, he was worthier by far than Yao or Shun.' Zigong said, 'By observing a ruler's rituals, he knew his government; by hearing his music, he knew his Virtue. After an interval of a hundred generations he could rank the kings of those hundred generations, without one of them eluding his judgment. Since the beginning of human life there has never been another Confucius.' You Ruo said, 'Is it only among human beings that we find this? It is true as well of the unicorn among animals, the phoenix among birds, Mount Tai among hills, and rivers and oceans among flowing waters; they are all of a kind. So, too, is the sage of the same kind as other people. Yet he emerges from among his kind and rises to a higher level. Since the beginning of human life, there has never been one greater than Confucius.'"

A3] Mencius said, "One who, supported by force, pretends to being humane is a hegemon, and a hegemon has to have a large state. One who out of Virtue practices humaneness is a true king, and a true king does not need anything large. Tang did it with only seventy *li*, and King Wen did it with a hundred.

"When one uses force to make people submit, they do not submit in their hearts but only because their strength is insufficient. When one uses Virtue to make people submit, they are pleased to the depths of their hearts, and they sincerely submit. So it was with the seventy disciples who submitted to Confucius. The ode says,

> From the west, and from the east,
> From the south and from the north,
> No one thought of not submitting.[9]

This is what was meant."

A4] Mencius said, "One who is humane will be distinguished; one who is inhumane will be disgraced. Now, to dislike disgrace yet abide in inhumanity is like disliking dampness yet abiding in a low place. If one dislikes disgrace, there is nothing better than to honor Virtue and to esteem men of service, giving positions to the worthy and offices to the capable. When the state is at peace, one should use the occasion to examine his administration and laws, and even the great states must surely be impressed. The ode says,

> Before the heavens darkened with rain,
> I gathered bark from the mulberry tree,
> Weaving it closely in my window and door.
> Now among those people below,
> Who will dare to insult me?[10]

---

9. Ode 244 (Legge, *Chinese Classics*, 4:460–64).

10. Ode 155. The poem is written in the voice of a little bird that has been molested by the larger kite owl (ibid., 4:233–35).

Confucius said, 'Surely the one who made this poem must have known the Way. If a ruler is able to govern his state well, who will dare to insult him?' But now in states that are at peace they take the occasion to abandon themselves to pleasure and indulge in idleness, thus seeking calamities for themselves. Whether calamities or happiness—these are always the result of one's own seeking. The ode says,

> Be ever thoughtful, and worthy of the ordinance,
> Thus seeking for yourself much happiness.[11]

This is what is meant by the "Taijia" when it says,

> When Heaven makes misfortunes,
> It is still possible to escape them.
> When the misfortunes are of our own making,
> It is no longer possible to live."[12]

[2A5] Mencius said, "When a ruler honors those who are exemplary and employs those who are capable, so that outstanding persons hold positions of authority, all the world's scholars will be pleased and will want to stand in his court. When in his marketplace he levies a ground rent, but without levying a tax on goods, or else enforces the regulations but without levying any ground rent, all the world's merchants will be pleased and will want to store their goods in his marketplace. When at his frontier passes there is an inspection but no tax is levied, all the world's travelers will be pleased and will want to travel on his roads. When tillers are required to render their assistance[13] but are not taxed, then all the world's farmers will be pleased and will want to till his fields. When individuals are not fined and no levy of cloth is exacted,[14]

---

11. Ode 235 (Legge, *The Chinese Classics*, 4:427–31).

12. See the "Taijia" section of the *Classic of Documents*, in ibid., 3:207.

13. This appears to be a reference to the mutual assistance owed under the well-field, discussed in 3A3.

14. The meaning of this passage is unclear. Some commentators refer to the *Rites of Zhou* (*Zhou li* 周禮), which indicates that fines were imposed on those who did not do sufficient work as well as a tax, levied in cloth, on families that failed to plant a required number of mulberry trees.

all the world's people will be pleased and will want to reside within his state. If one is truly able to do these five things, the people of neighboring states will look to him as a father and mother and follow him like his children. Never, since the birth of humankind, has anyone ever succeeded in causing people to attack their parents. So the ruler will have no enemies in the world, and one who has no enemies in the world is the agent of Heaven. Could he then fail to become a true king?"

6] Mencius said, "All human beings have a mind that cannot bear to see the sufferings of others. The ancient kings had such a commiserating mind and, accordingly, a commiserating government. Having a commiserating mind, and effecting a commiserating government, governing the world was like turning something around on the palm of the hand.

"Here is why I say that all human beings have a mind that commiserates with others. Now, if anyone were suddenly to see a child about to fall into a well, his mind would be filled with alarm, distress, pity, and compassion. That he would react accordingly is not because he would hope to use the opportunity to ingratiate himself with the child's parents, nor because he would seek commendation from neighbors and friends, nor because he would hate the adverse reputation [that could come from not reacting accordingly]. From this it may be seen that one who lacks a mind that feels pity and compassion would not be human; one who lacks a mind that feels shame and aversion would not be human; one who lacks a mind that feels modesty and compliance would not be human; and one who lacks a mind that knows right and wrong would not be human.

"The mind's feeling of pity and compassion is the sprout of humaneness [*ren* 仁]; the mind's feeling of shame and aversion is the sprout of rightness [*yi* 義]; the mind's feeling of modesty and compliance is the sprout of propriety [*li* 禮]; and the mind's sense of right and wrong is the sprout of wisdom [*zhi* 智].

"Human beings have these four sprouts just as they have four limbs. For one to have these four sprouts and yet to say of oneself that one is unable to fulfill them is to injure oneself, while to say that one's ruler is unable to fulfill them is to injure one's ruler. When we know how to enlarge and bring to fulfillment these four sprouts that are within us, it will be like a fire beginning to burn or a spring finding an outlet. If one is able to bring them to fulfillment, they will be sufficient to enable him to protect 'all within the four seas'; if one is not, they will be insufficient even to enable him to serve his parents."

[2A7] Mencius said, "Is the maker of arrows less humane than the maker of armor? The maker of arrows fears only that people will not be hurt; the maker of armor fears only that people will be hurt. This is so also in the case of the priest and the coffin maker. Therefore one must be mindful in choosing one's occupation.

"Confucius said, 'It is humaneness that makes a neighborhood beautiful. If in deciding on one's dwelling one does not dwell in humaneness, how can he be wise?'[15] Humaneness is the honor conferred by Heaven and is a person's peaceful abode. No one can cause us not to be humane—rather, this derives from a lack of wisdom. One who is neither humane nor wise, who is devoid of ritual propriety and rightness, will be the servant of others. To be the servant of others yet ashamed of his service is like the maker of bows who is ashamed of making bows or the maker of arrows who is ashamed of making arrows. If one is ashamed of this, there is nothing better than to be humane. One who would be humane is like the archer. The archer corrects his position and then shoots. If he shoots and misses he does not blame those who are more adept than he; rather, he turns within and seeks within himself."

[2A8] Mencius said, "Zilu, when told that he had made a mistake, was happy. Yu, when he heard good words, bowed. The great Shun was greater still. He regarded goodness as something he shared with the people; he relinquished his own way to follow others; he took pleasure in learning from others how to be good. From the time he was a farmer, a potter, or a fisherman to the time he was emperor, he always learned from others. To learn from others how to be good is to be good together with them. Thus, of the attributes of the noble man there is none greater than his being good together with others."

[2A9] Boyi, if he did not approve of a ruler, he would not serve him. If he did not approve of a friend, he would not remain friends with him. He

15. *Analects* 4:1.

would not stand in the court of a bad person, nor would he speak with a bad person. For him to stand in the court of a bad person or to speak with a bad person would have been like sitting in dirt and soot with his court robes and his court cap on. This mentality of disliking anything bad went to the point that if he were standing with a villager whose cap was not on straight he would depart directly, as if he were about to be defiled. Therefore, although some of the lords approached him with excellent messages, he would not receive them; he refused to receive them because it was beneath his dignity to be associated with them.

Liuxia Hui was not ashamed of an impure ruler, nor did he disdain a minor office. When he was advanced, he did not conceal his abilities but resolutely carried out his Way. When he was passed over, he did not complain; when he was afflicted with poverty, he did not grieve. So it was that he said, 'You are you, and I am I. If you were to stand by my side in a state of complete undress, how could you cause me to be defiled?' Thus he was completely at ease in the presence of others yet never lost himself. When he was urged to remain, he would remain. The reason that when urged to remain he would remain was that it was beneath his dignity to depart."

Mencius said, "Boyi was constrained, while Liuxia Hui was undignified. Neither should be followed by the noble person."

so does Mencius believe in a middle path between Boyi & Liuxia Hui?

BOOK 2B

[2B1] Mencius said, "Heaven's seasons are less crucial than earth's advantages, and earth's advantages less crucial than human accord. There is a city with an inner wall of three *li* in circumference and an outer wall of seven *li*: it may be surrounded and attacked but cannot be taken. To surround and attack it requires Heaven's seasonableness; that it cannot be taken is because Heaven's seasons are less crucial than earth's advantages. There is another city: it is not that its walls are not high, it moats deep, its weapons potent, or its food supply abundant, but it must be abandoned because earth's advantages are less crucial than human accord. Therefore it is said, 'A people is not bounded by the limits of its borders; a state is not secured by the ruggedness of its mountains and valleys; the world is not awed by the sharpness of its weapons.'

"One who attains the Way has many to assist him; one who loses the Way has few. One who is assisted by a few ultimately finds that he is abandoned even by his relatives, while one who is assisted by many ultimately finds that he is followed by the whole world. When he uses the strength of one who is followed by the whole world to attack one who has been abandoned even by his own relatives, the noble person may not need to fight, or, if he does fight, he will surely prevail."

[2B2] Mencius was about to go to court to see the king when the king sent someone to say, "I would have liked to come to see you, but, having a cold, cannot be exposed to the wind. In the morning I shall hold court and wonder whether it will be possible to see you?"

Mencius replied, "Unfortunately, I am ill and cannot come to court."

The next day, as Mencius was setting out on a condolence visit to the Dongguo family, Gongsun Chou said, "Yesterday you excused yourself on ground of illness, while today you are undertaking a visit of condolence. Surely your action must be improper in either one case or the other?"[1]

Mencius said, "Yesterday I was ill; today I am better. Why should I not pay this visit of condolence?"

The king sent someone to inquire about Mencius's illness; a doctor came as well. Meng Zhongzi[2] replied, saying, "Yesterday, when the king's order arrived, he had a slight illness and could not come to court. Today his illness is a little better, and he hastened to go to court. I do not know whether or not he was able to get there."

He sent several persons to look for Mencius along the road and say to him, "Please by all means go to court before returning home."

Mencius felt obliged to go to spend the night at Jing Chou's. Master Jing said, "Within the family there is the relation between father and son; without, there is the relation between ruler and minister. These are the greatest of human relations. The relation between father and son is based on kindness [*en* 恩]; the relation between ruler and minister, on respect [*jing* 敬]. I have seen the king's respect for the Master but have yet to see the Master's respect for the king."

Mencius said, "What do you mean by saying such a thing? Among the people of Qi there are none who speak to the king of humaneness and rightness. Could it be that they find that humaneness and rightness are not admirable? Rather, in their hearts they say, 'This is not a fit person with whom to discuss humaneness and rightness.' There is no greater lack of respect than this. I dare not set forth before the king anything but the Way of Yao and Shun, and therefore there is no one among the people of Qi who respects the king as much as I do."

Master Jing said, "No, this is not what I meant. It says in the *Book of Rites*, 'When the father calls, the response should be immediate. When the ruler commands, there may be no waiting for a carriage.'[3] You were indeed going to court when you heard the king's command, but then you did not go. It would seem that this was not consistent with the rites."

---

1. That is, either Mencius should not have pleaded illness yesterday, or he should not have undertaken the condolence visit today.

2. Apparently one of Mencius's relatives.

3. Passages similar in content to what is quoted here are found in the "Quli 曲禮" chapter of the *Book of Rites*.

Mencius said, "How can you say this? Zengzi said, 'The wealth of Jin and Chu cannot be equaled. They have their wealth; I have my humaneness. They have their rank; I have my rightness. Why should I feel dissatisfied?' Since Zengzi said this, how could it not be right? Though the Way is one, there are three things in the world that are universally honored: one is rank, one is age, and one is Virtue. At court, rank is most important; in the villages, it is age; in caring for the world and looking after the people, it is Virtue. How can having one of these be regarded as cause for belittling the other two?

"Therefore a ruler who is to accomplish great deeds must have ministers whom he does not just summon. When he wishes to consult them he goes to them. If he does not honor Virtue and delight in the Way to this extent, then it is not worth associating with him. Thus there was the relation between Tang and Yi Yin: Tang learned of him and then he made him a minister, after which he had no trouble becoming a true king. There was the relation between Duke Huan and Guan Zhong: Duke Huan heard of him and then he made him a minister, after which he had no trouble becoming a hegemon.

"In the world of today the territories of the states are equal and the Virtue of their rulers is comparable, with none being able to excel among the others. They like to make ministers of those whom they teach and do not like to make ministers of those by whom they may be taught. Tang's relation with Yi Yin and Duke Huan's relation with Guan Zhong were such that they did not dare summon them [but went to them instead]. If even Guan Zhong could not be summoned, how much less so one who would not be a Guan Zhong."[4]

[2B3] Chen Zhen asked, "On a former occasion, when you were in Qi, the king sent a hundred *yi*,[5] which you did not accept. You did, however, accept seventy *yi* sent to you while you were in Song and fifty *yi* sent to you while you were in Xie. If it was right not to accept what was

---

4. See 2A1.

5. Yi 鎰 was the name of a mint town in Qi during this period and apparently also a unit of currency. See Wang Yuquan, *Early Chinese Coinage*, 187, cited in W. A. C. H. Dobson, trans., *Mencius* (Toronto: University of Toronto Press, 1963), 198.

sent on the prior occasion, then to have accepted what was sent on the subsequent occasions must have been wrong. If accepting on the subsequent occasions was right, then not accepting on the prior occasion must have been wrong. Surely you must resolve this one way or the other."

Mencius said, "It was right in each case. When I was in Song, I was about to undertake a long journey, and a traveler must be sent off with a parting gift. The message said, 'Sent as a parting gift.' How could I not have accepted it? When I was in Xie, my mind was occupied with the need for safety precautions. The message said, 'Having heard of the need for precautions, I am sending this to provide for protection.' How could I not have accepted it? When I was in Qi, there was no occasion for a gift, and to send someone a gift in the absence of any occasion for it is bribery. Is it possible to procure a noble person with a bribe?"

4] When Mencius went to Pinglu,[6] he said to its governor, Kong Juxin, "If you had a lancer who broke rank three times in a single day, would you get rid of him or not?"

The answer was, "I would not wait for the third time."

Yet you, sir, have also 'broken rank' many times. In disastrous years, in years of famine, thousands of your people who were old and weak were left to tumble over into drains and ditches, while those who were strong were scattered in the four directions."

"This is not something that is within my capacity to control!"

"Now here is a person who accepts the responsibility for another man's oxen and sheep, and, as he is supposed to care for them, he must search for pasture and fodder. But if, though he searches, he cannot find pasture and fodder, shall he return them to their owner or stand by and watch them die?"

"In this I have been at fault."

Another day Mencius went to see the king and said, "I know five of the persons who govern towns in your state, and the only one who recognizes his faults is Kong Juxin—and he recounted the story for the king.

---

6. A border town in the state of Qi.

The king said, "In this it is I who am at fault."

[2B5] Mencius said to Chi Wa, "It would seem that when you declined the governorship of Lingqiu and asked to be made chief judge,[7] it was so that you would be able to speak out. Now several months have passed. Have you not yet been able to speak?"

Chi Wa remonstrated with the king, and, when his advice was not followed, he resigned his office and departed.

There was a man of Qi who said, "When he was deciding on behalf of Chi Wa, Mencius did well enough, but when it comes to deciding about himself, I do not know."

When Gongduzi[8] told this to Mencius, he replied, "I have heard that one who holds an office will resign if he cannot fulfill his duties. He resigns if he has the responsibility for speaking out but cannot speak. I hold no office, nor have I the responsibility for speaking out. Why should I not have the latitude to decide freely whether to remain or to retire?"

[2B6] When Mencius was a high official in Qi, he went to Teng on a mission of condolence,[9] and the king appointed the governor of Ke, Wang Huan, to assist him. Wang Huan was in attendance morning and night, but in the course of the journey from Qi to Teng and back again, Mencius never once spoke with him about the purpose of the mission on which they were engaged. Gongsun Chou said, "Your position as an official of Qi is hardly a minor one, nor is the road from Qi to Teng short. Why is it that at no point in the journey there and back again did you ever speak with him about the mission on which you were engaged?" Mencius replied, "There were others who were in charge of these matters. What need had I to speak of them?"

[2B7] Mencius went from Qi to Lu to bury his mother and, on his return to Qi, stopped in Ying. Chung Yu asked, "On a former occasion, not

---

7. Following Charles O. Hucker's translation of *shishi* 士師 in *A Dictionary of Official Titles in Imperial China* (Stanford, Calif.: Stanford University Press, 1985), 428, s. v. entry 5299.
8. A disciple of Mencius's.
9. To be present for the obsequies of Duke Wen of Teng.

realizing my lack of capacity, you appointed me to oversee the making of the coffins. Under the circumstances I did not presume to ask, yet now humbly request to inquire about this: it seemed that the wood was too fine."

Mencius said, "In antiquity there were no rules concerning the inner or the outer coffin. In middle antiquity both the inner and the outer coffins were supposed to be seven inches thick, and this was true for everyone from the Son of Heaven to the common people. This was not simply for the sake of a beautiful appearance but because it allowed, at the last, for the full expression of people's hearts. If people were not permitted to do this, they could not feel satisfaction, and if they did not have the means to do it, they also could not feel satisfaction. The ancients, if they were able to do this, and had the means to do it, all employed this practice. Why should I alone not have done so? Moreover, is it not a comfort to the mind to keep the earth from touching the bodies of those we love who have been transformed in death? I have heard that the noble person would not for anything in the world stint when it came to his parents.

8] In a private conversation Shen Tong asked, "May the state of Yan be chastised?"[10]

Mencius said, "It may. Zikuai was not entitled to give Yan to someone else, nor was Zizhi entitled to receive Yan from Zikuai.[11] Suppose there were an officer here and that you were pleased with him. Suppose that, without informing the king, you took it upon yourself to give this officer your own emolument and rank and that he, again without the king's order, took it upon himself to receive them from you. Would this be acceptable? And how would it be any different from what happened in Yan?"[12]

---

10. That is, can Yan be attacked as a punishment?

11. Zikuai, the ruler of the state of Yan, offered the rulership to his minister, Zizhi, apparently not suspecting that Zizhi would accept. He did. Mencius faults both men for improper behavior.

12. There is, of course, a difference in that the actions of the ruler of Yan at least had the royal endorsement (his own) that the two officers in Mencius's hypothetical case did not have.

The people of Qi did chastise Yan.

Someone asked Mencius, "Did you actually advise Qi to chastise Yan?" Mencius replied, "No. Shen Tong asked whether Yan might be chastised; I replied that it might. They went ahead and attacked it. Had he asked, 'Who may chastise it?' I would have replied that a minister appointed by Heaven might chastise it. Now suppose there were a murderer. If someone asked, 'May he be put to death?' I would reply that he might. If he asked, 'Who may put him to death?' I would reply that the chief judge might put him to death. How would I have advised that one Yan should chastise another Yan?"[13]

[2B9] The people of Yan having rebelled, the king of Qi said, "I am deeply ashamed to confront Mencius."

Chen Jia said, "The king should not be troubled about this. Whom does the king consider more humane and wise—himself or the Duke of Zhou?" The king said, "What kind of question is that?"

Chen Jia said, "The Duke of Zhou appointed Guanshu to oversee Yin, but Guanshu used Yin to stage a rebellion. If he appointed him while knowing this, he cannot have been humane. If he appointed him without knowing it, he was not wise. If the Duke of Zhou was not completely humane or completely wise, how much less could anyone expect this of the king? I beg leave to go to see Mencius and explain this."

He went to see Mencius and asked, "What kind of man was the Duke of Zhou?"

Mencius replied, "He was a sage of antiquity"

Did it happen that he appointed Guanshu to oversee Yin and that Guanshu used Yin to stage a rebellion?"

"It did."

"Did the Duke of Zhou appoint him knowing that he would rebel?"

"He did not know."

"Then even sages make mistakes?"

"The Duke of Zhou was the younger brother; Guanshu was the older brother. Was not the Duke of Zhou's mistake at the same time also

---

13. In other words, Qi, being much like Yan in terms of the quality of its government, was not a suitable agent to intervene in Yan.

correct? Besides, when the noble persons of antiquity made mistakes, they corrected them, whereas the noble persons of today persist in their errors. The mistakes of the noble persons of antiquity were like eclipses of the sun and moon. The people could all see them. Once they had corrected these mistakes, the people all looked up to them.[14] And do the noble persons of today only persist in their mistakes? No, they also go on to make excuses for them."

10] Having resigned his office, Mencius was returning home. The king came to see him and said, "In the past, I wanted to see you but could not. Then, to my great delight, I got to serve with you in the same court. But now you are once again about to abandon me and return home. I do not know whether in time to come I may be able to see you again?"

Mencius replied, "Though I did not presume to ask, this is certainly what I would wish."

Another day the king said to Shizi, "I would like to give Mencius a house in the middle of the state and a stipend of ten thousand *zhong*[15] to support his disciples, so that the officers and all the people of the state will have an example to honor and emulate. How would it be if you, sir, were to speak with him about this for me?"

Shizi relied on Chenzi[16] to inform Mencius. When Chenzi reported Shizi's words to Mencius, Mencius said, "Very well, but how could someone like Shizi know that this is impossible? Perhaps he supposes that I am one who desires wealth. Would one desirous of wealth decline a hundred thousand in order to accept ten thousand?

"Ji Sun said, 'How strange was Zishu Yi! He promoted himself to serve in government, but as his counsel was not followed, he had to retire. He then promoted his own son and younger brother to serve as high officials. Who is there who does not desire wealth and honor? But in the midst of wealth and honor he alone had his own private "high mound."'

---

14. The preceding three sentences are very close to the *Analects* 19:21.

15. A *zhong* 鍾 was a measure of volume, in this case for an official allowance of grain.

16. According to Zhao Qi's commentary, Chenzi was Chen Zhen, a disciple of Mencius's, who appears in 2B3.

"In antiquity the markets existed for the purpose of allowing people to exchange what they had for what they lacked, and the officials simply supervised it. But there was a greedy fellow who would seek out a 'high mound' and climb it, looking right and left in order to capture all the profit in the market. People all found him greedy, and so they taxed him. The taxing of merchants began with that greedy fellow."

[2B11] After he left Qi, Mencius was lodging in Zhou[17] when a person who wished to detain him on behalf of the king sat down and spoke to him. Mencius did not respond but leaned on his armrest and went to sleep. The guest was not pleased and said, "Only after passing the night in fasting did I dare to speak, but you sleep and do not listen. You must pardon me if I do not request any further interviews with you."

Mencius said, "Sit down; I will make this clear to you. In the time of Duke Mu of Lu,[18] unless the duke had kept someone at Zisi's[19] side, he could not have assured Zisi's peace of mind. And unless Xie Liu[20] and Shen Xiang[21] had someone at Duke Mu's side, he could not have assured their sense of security. You, sir, are concerned about me, yet not to the point where you treat me as Zisi was treated. Are you breaking with me or am I breaking with you?"

[2B12] After Mencius had left Qi, Yin Shi said to someone, "If he *did not know* that the king could not become a Tang or a Wu,[22] then he was not very bright, and if he *knew* that he could not and came anyway, then he was seeking his own enrichment. He came a thousand *li* to see a king and, having failed, he left. But it took him three nights before he got beyond Zhou—how slow and reluctant was this departure! I am most disappointed about this."

---

17. A town in the southwest of Qi.

18. Known as Duke Xian, he ruled in Lu from the late fifth to the early fourth centuries B.C.E.

19. Zisi was the grandson of Confucius. The idea is that someone had to be with Zisi to assure him of the duke's respect and regard.

20. An official who served under Duke Mu, he is referred to in 3B7 and again, under the name Ziliu, in 6B6.

21. According to some sources, he was the son of Confucius's disciple Zizhang.

22. Reputed founders of the Shang and Zhou dynasties, respectively.

When Gaozi[23] reported this, Mencius said, "How could someone like Yin Shi understand me? I came a thousand *li* to see a king. This was what I desired to do. But, having failed, I left. How could this have been what I desired to do? I could do nothing else. When I spent three nights before leaving Zhou, in my own mind this still was departing in haste. I was hoping that the king would change. Had he changed, he would have recalled me. Only after I had left Zhou without the king's having recalled me did I have an overwhelming compulsion to return home.

"Even so, how can it be said that I abandoned the king? The king is still able to do good. If the king were to use me, could it happen that this would bring peace to the people of Qi only? The people of the entire world would be at peace. I am hoping that the king will change. Daily I look forward to this.

"How could I be like the small people who remonstrate with their ruler and, when their remonstration is not accepted, become angry. They then depart, their faces full of rage, and exhaust all their strength traveling for an entire day before stopping for the night."

When Yin Shi heard this he said, "I am truly a small person."

[3] As Mencius was departing Qi, Chong Yu questioned him along the way, saying, "From your expression it would seem that you are unhappy. Yet on a former occasion I heard you [quoting Confucius] say, 'The noble person neither repines against Heaven nor reproaches men.'"[24]

"That age was one time; this is another.[25] In five hundred years a true king should appear, and in between there should be men renowned in their generation. From the beginning of the Zhou it has been more than seven hundred years. Given that number, the time is past due,

23. Not the Gaozi of 2A2 or of 6A1–4 and 6A6, but a disciple whose name is written with a different Chinese character. See also 6B3, 7B21, and 7B22.

24. The quote is from the *Analects* 14:37.

25. That is to say, the time when Confucius first said the line that Chong Yu recounts is different from the current age. Mencius is not saying the line Chong Yu cites is *inapplicable* in his case, which is what readers will be misled to think from most English translations of this passage. Instead, Mencius introduces a short discourse on how their historical situation differs from that of Confucius. His *point* is that in this later age, the coming of a sage or great worthy is far past due. Given that there is no one else but Mencius to fulfill such roles, *why would he be unhappy?* See 7B38.

and considering the circumstances, it is still possible. Heaven does not yet want to bring peace to the world. If it wanted to bring peace to the world, who is there in the present age apart from me? Why should I be unhappy?"[26]

[2B14]   After Mencius left Qi, he lived in Xiu. Gongsong Chou asked him, "Was it the way in antiquity to serve in office without receiving an emolument?"

"No. When I had an audience with the king in Chong, my intention had been to withdraw and to leave. I had no inclination to change my intention, and therefore I received no salary. Then there was an order for the mobilization of troops, and it was not possible to request permission to leave. To remain long in Qi had not been my intention."

---

26. Some commentators have suggested that the attitude toward Heaven revealed in this passage is similar to the attitude of Confucius expressed in the *Analects* 9:5: "If Heaven had intended to destroy this culture, later mortals would not have been able to share in it. And if Heaven is not going to destroy this culture, what can the people of Kuang do to me?"

BOOK 3A

[1] Duke Wen of Teng, Shizi,[1] on his way to Chu, passed by Song in order to see Mencius. Mencius spoke about human nature being good, constantly commending Yao and Shun.[2] When Shizi was returning from Chu, he again went to see Mencius.

Mencius said, "Do you doubt my words? The Way is one and one only."

Cheng Jian said to Duke Jing of Qi, "They were men. I too am a man. Why need I be in awe of them?"

Yan Yuan[3] said, "What kind of man was Shun? What kind of man am I? One who exerts effort will also be like them."

Gongming Yi said, "King Wen is my teacher. How could the Duke of Zhou deceive me?"

"Now, given its length and breadth, Teng must be around fifty *li*—still large enough that it can make a good state. The *Classic of Documents* says: 'If the medicine does not induce dizziness, it will not cure the illness.'"[4]

[2] Duke Ding of Teng[5] died. Shizi said to Ran You.[6] "Long ago in Song Mencius spoke with me, and what he said has always remained in my heart; I have never forgotten it. Now, to my sorrow, I come upon "the

---

1. Duke Wen was a posthumous name; Shizi was the name by which he was known at the time he was heir apparent.
2. The sage-kings of antiquity. See also 5A.
3. Confucius's favorite disciple.
4. "The Charge to Yue," part 1, *Classic of Documents*, in Legge, *Chinese Classics*, 3:252. In this passage, the king asks the minister to be like medicine to him.
5. The father of Duke Wen.
6. His tutor.

great affair."[7] Before I carry out this undertaking, I would like to send you to inquire of Mencius."

Ran You went to Zou and asked Mencius. Mencius said, "Is this not good too? In carrying out the funeral arrangements for parents one exerts oneself to the fullest. Zengzi said, 'When they are alive, serve them according to ritual; when they die, bury them according to ritual and sacrifice to them according to ritual.[8] This is called "filial devotion."' I have not learned about the sacrifices pertaining to the various lords. But I have heard this: in the three years' mourning, the garment of coarse cloth and the diet of rice gruel were shared in common by the three dynasties and extended to everyone from the Son of Heaven to the common people."

Ran You returned and reported on his mission, and the prince decided that the three years' mourning would be carried out. The family elders and the high officials did not concur in this and said, "None of the former princes of our ancestral house of Lu practiced this, nor did any of our former princes. For you to take it upon yourself to contravene what they did is unacceptable. Moreover, the *Record* says, 'In the observance of mourning and sacrifice, one follows the elders.'"[9] They said, "We have a source for this."

The prince said to Ran You, "In the past I was never given to study but was fond of horsemanship and swordplay. Now, the family elders and officers do not consider me adequate. I am afraid that I may be unable to exert myself to the fullest in carrying out this 'great affair of state.' I would like you to speak with Mencius on my behalf."

Ran You again went to Zou and inquired of Mencius. Mencius said, "This is so, but he cannot turn to anyone outside himself. Confucius said, 'When the lord dies his heir gives over authority to the chief minister.[10] He eats rice gruel. His face turns a deep black. As he approaches his position in the ceremony of mourning, he weeps. Among all the officers, none will dare not to grieve, following his example. What the

---

7. The death of a parent.
8. This part of the quotation is attributed to Confucius (*Analects* 2:5).
9. The text referred to here is not known.
10. Cf. the *Analects* 14:43.

one above loves, those below will care for still more deeply. 'The Virtue of the noble person is like the wind, and the Virtue of small people is like grass. When the wind blows over the grass, the grass must bend.'[11] Everything depends on the prince."

Ran You returned and reported on his mission. The prince said, "It is true: everything does indeed depend on me." For five months he dwelled in the mourning shed, issuing no orders or precepts. The officers and his clansmen acknowledged that he knew the rituals, and when it came time for the internment, people came from the four quarters to witness it. The mourners took great satisfaction from the sorrowfulness expressed in his countenance and the deep grief conveyed in his weeping.

A3]   Duke Wen of Teng asked about governing the state. Mencius replied, "The people's business may not be delayed. The ode says,

> In the morning gather the grasses,
> In the evening twist the ropes;
> Be quick to climb to the housetop,
> Begin to sow the hundred grains.[12]

The way of the people is this: that when they have a constant livelihood, they will have constant minds, but when they lack a constant livelihood, they will lack constant minds. When they lack constant minds, there is no dissoluteness, depravity, deviance, or excess to which they will not succumb. If, once they have sunk into crime, one responds by subjecting them to punishment—this is to entrap the people. When a humane man is in a position of authority, how could the entrapment of the people be allowed to occur?[13] Therefore, an exemplary ruler will be respectful, frugal, and reverent toward his subjects, and must take from the people only in accordance with the regulations. Yang Hu said, 'One

---

11. The last two sentences are close to a statement attributed to Confucius in the *Analects* 12:19.

12. Ode 154 (Legge, *Chinese Classics*, 3:226–33).

13. Mencius is recorded as having said almost exactly the same thing to King Xuan of Qi (see 1A7).

who would be wealthy will not be humane; one who would be humane will not be wealthy.'[14]

"The house of Xia mandated allotments of fifty *mu* and imposed the *gong* 貢 system. The Yin mandated allotments of seventy *mu* and instituted the *zhu* 助 system. The Zhou mandated allotments of one hundred *mu* and adopted the *che* 徹 system. Actually, the tax amounted in each case to one part in ten. *Che* means to share; *zhu* means to help. Master Long[15] said, 'In managing the land system there is nothing better than the *zhu*, nor worse than the *gong*.' With the *gong* system, the annual yield being averaged out over a number of years, the tax is rendered as a constant. In years of prosperity, when the grain crops are superabundant and more could be taken without causing any hardship, little is taken. In years of scarcity, when there is not enough left even to manure the fields, the full measure must be exacted. When one who is the father and mother of the people causes angry and sullen-looking people to have to borrow because, after a year of unremitting toil, they are still unable to nourish their parents—when he causes old people and young to be left to tumble over into drains and ditches—how can he be regarded as a father and mother to the people?

"Now, Teng assuredly has the practice of providing salaries for hereditary officials. Yet the ode says,

> May the rain fall on our public fields,
> So, too, on our private fields.[16]

Only in the *zhu* system is there the idea of public fields, and, viewed from this perspective, we may see that Zhou, too, practiced the *zhu* system.

14. Yang Hu (or Yang Huo) is the person whose interactions with Confucius are recorded in the *Analects* 17:2 and, again, in *Mencius* 3B7. When Confucius declined to see Yang, out of dismay at his role as a minister to the Ji clan in the state of Lu, Yang sent him a pig, imposing on Confucius the ritual requirement to visit Yang to express his appreciation. Since Yang is represented as an unsavory and conniving character, commentators puzzle over the fact that he is quoted in the *Mencius* as having made what appears to be an appropriate statement about humaneness.

15. Master Long is identified by Zhao Qi only as "a virtuous man of antiquity." He is quoted again in 6A7.

16. Ode 212. In James Legge's translation, the lines read, "May it rain first on our public fields, / And then come to our private!" (*Chinese Classics*, 4:380–82).

"Establish the *xiang*, the *xu*, the *xue* 學, and the *xiao* 校 so as to teach them.[17] The *xiang* is for nourishing, the *xiao* for instruction, the *xu* is for archery. The Xia used the term *xiao*; the Yin used the term *xu*; the Zhou used the term *xiang*. All three used the term *xue*. And all were designed to clarify human relations. When human relations are clarified by those above, the little people will live in affection below. If a true king should arise, he will surely come and find in you an example, and you will be the teacher of a king. The ode says,

> Zhou is an old state,
> But its mandate is new.[18]

This speaks of King Wen. You must practice these things with all your strength; this will indeed serve to renew your state."

The duke sent Bi Zhan to inquire about the well-field system. Mencius said, "Since your lord intends to practice humane government, and you have been selected by him for employment, he must put forth great effort. Now, humane government must begin with the setting of boundaries. If the boundaries are not set correctly, the division of the land into well-fields will not be equal, and the grain allowances for official emoluments will not be equitable. This is why harsh rulers and corrupt officials are prone to neglect the setting of boundaries. Once the boundaries have been set correctly, the division of the fields and the determination of emoluments can be settled without difficulty. Now, while the territory of Teng is narrow and small, it has both noble men and country people. Without noble men, there would be no one to rule the country people, and, without the country people, there would be no one to feed the noble men.

"Please allow that in the countryside one square of land out of nine should be used for mutual aid. In the capital, the people should assess themselves with a tax amounting to one part in ten. From the highest officers on down, everyone must have a *gui* field,[19] and that *gui* field

---

17 See 1A3, n. 9.

18. Ode 235 (Legge, *Chinese Classics*, 4:427–31).

19. Officials received a *gui* 圭 field, the income from which was to be used to support the conduct of sacrifices.

should be fifty *mu*. Remaining males should have twenty-five *mu*. Neither at the occasion of a death nor of a change of a residence should people leave the village. When those in a village who hold land in the same well-field befriend one another in their going out and their coming in, assist one another in their protection and defense, and sustain one another through illness and distress, the hundred surnames[20] will live together in affection and harmony.

"A square *li* constitutes a well-field, and the well-field contains nine hundred *mu*. The central plot among them is a public field, and eight families each have private holdings of a hundred *mu*. Together they cultivate the public field, and only when the public work is done do they dare attend to their private work, this being what distinguishes the country people. This is the general outline, the details of which will be up to the ruler and you."

[3A4] Xu Xing, who espoused the views of Shennong,[21] came from Chu to Teng. Going directly to the gate, he announced to Duke Wen, "I am a man from distant parts, who has heard that you practice humane government and wish to receive land to live on so as to become your subject." Duke Wen gave him a place to live. Xu Xing's followers, numbering several tens, all wore clothing of unwoven hemp, made sandals, and wove mats for a living.

Chen Liang's follower, Chen Xiang, along with his brother Xin, came with their ploughs on their backs from Song to Teng. They said, "Having heard that you practice sagely government and are also a sage, we wish to become your subjects."

When Chen Xiang met Xu Xing, he was extremely pleased and, completely abandoning what he had learned before, became his disciple. When Chen Xiang met Mencius, he recounted the words of Xu Xing, saying, "The lord of Teng is truly an exemplary ruler; however, he has not yet heard the Way. The exemplary man works alongside the people and eats what they eat. He prepares his own meals, morning and

---

20. That is, the people as a whole.

21. Shennong (the Divine Farmer) was associated with the agriculturalist tradition. For a revealing study of this tradition, see A. C. Graham, "The *Nung-chia* 'School of Tillers' and the Origins of Peasant Utopianism in China," *BOAS* 42, no. 1 (1979): 66–100.

evening, while at the same time he governs. Now, Teng has granaries and treasuries. This is for the ruler to burden the people in order to nourish himself. How can he be called an exemplary man?"

Mencius said, "Master Xu must only eat the grain that he has planted himself?"

"Yes."

"And Master Xu must wear only cloth that he has woven himself?"

"No, Master Xu wears unwoven hemp."

"Does Master Xu wear a cap?"

"He wears a cap."

"What kind of cap?"

"His cap is plain."

"Does he weave it himself?"

"No, he exchanges grain for it."

"Why does Master Xu not weave it himself?"

"That would interfere with his tilling the soil."

"Does Master Xu use an iron cauldron and an earthenware pot to cook his food, and does he till his fields with iron implements?"

"Yes."

"Does he make them himself?"

"No, he exchanges grain for them."

"To exchange grain for these various implements and utensils is not to burden the potter or the founder, nor could the potter and the founder, in exchanging their implements and utensils for grain, be burdening the agriculturalist. Then why doesn't Master Xu become a potter and a founder so that he can obtain everything he uses from his own household? Why does he go about this way and that trading and exchanging with the various craftsmen? Why does Master Xu not spare himself the trouble?"

"The work of the craftsman definitely cannot be carried on simultaneously with the work of tilling the soil."

"Then is governing the world unique in that this alone can be carried out simultaneously with the work of tilling the soil? There are the affairs of the great man, and the affairs of the small man. In the case of any individual person, the things that the craftsmen make are available to him; if each person had to make everything he needed for his own use, the world would be full of people chasing after one another on the roads. Therefore it is said, 'Some labor with their minds, while others labor with their strength. Those who labor with their minds govern others, while those who labor with their strength are governed by others. Those who are governed by others support them; those who govern others are supported by them.' The rightness of this is universally acknowledged in the world.

inequality is natural & inevitable

"In the time of Yao the world was not yet settled. The waters of the deluge overran their channels, and the world was inundated. Grasses and trees were luxuriant; birds and beasts proliferated. The five grains could not be grown. Birds and beasts crowded in on people, and the prints of the beasts and the tracks of the birds crisscrossed each other throughout the Middle Kingdom. Yao alone[22] grieved anxiously over this. He elevated Shun to institute the regulations of government, and Shun employed Yi to manage fire. Yi set fire to the mountains and marshes and burned them, and the birds and beasts fled into hiding. Yu dredged out the nine rivers. He cleared the courses of the Qi and the Ta, leading them to flow to the sea, opened the way for the Ru and the Han, and guided the courses of the Huai and the Si, leading them to flow to the Yangtze.[23] Only then could those in the Middle Kingdom [cultivate the land and] eat. During that time, Yu was abroad in the land for eight years. Three times he passed his own door but did not enter. Although he may have wanted to cultivate the fields, could he have done so?

"Hou Ji[24] taught the people to sow and to reap and to cultivate the five grains. When the grains ripened, the people had their nourishment. It is the way of human beings that when they have sufficient food, warm clothing, and comfortable dwellings, but are without education, they become little more than birds and beasts. It was the part

22. Yao alone because he was a sage-ruler who could anticipate the potential progress of human civilization.

23. The twelfth-century scholar Zhu Xi and, following him, James Legge have pointed out that there are problems with the geography here. Zhu Xi explains it as an error on the part of the recorder of Mencius's words (Zhu Xi, *Sishu jizhu*, commentary on *Mencius* 3A:4; and Legge, *Chinese Classics*, 2:251).

24. Shun's minister of agriculture. See also 4B29.

of the sage[25] to grieve anxiously over this. He appointed Xie minister of education in order to teach people about human relations: that
between parents and children there is affection; between ruler and minister, rightness; between husband and wife, separate functions; between
older and younger, proper order; and between friends, faithfulness.
Fangxun[26] said,

> Encourage them, lead them,
> Reform them, correct them,
> Assist them, give them wings,[27]
> Let them "get it for themselves."[28]
> Then follow by inspiring them to Virtue.

How could the sages, who were so anxious about the people, have the
leisure to till the soil? What caused anxiety for Yao was the thought of
not getting Shun [as his successor]; what caused anxiety for Shun was
the thought of not getting Yu and Gao Yao. The one whose anxiety is
caused by a plot of one hundred *mu* not being properly cultivated is
a farmer.

"To share one's wealth with others is called kindness. To teach others to be good is called loyalty. To find the right man for the empire is
called humaneness. Thus, to give the empire to someone is easy, whereas
to find the right man for the empire is difficult. Confucius said, 'Great
indeed was Yao as a ruler. Only Heaven is great, and yet Yao patterned
himself after Heaven. How vast, how magnificent! The people could find
no name for it. What a ruler was Shun! How lofty, how majestic! He possessed the empire as if it were nothing to him.'[29] As Yao and Shun ruled

---

25. That is, Shun.

26. That is, Yao, who is referred to by this term in the *Classic of Documents*. Legge has
doubts that this refers to Yao, though Zhu Xi, whose interpretation Legge usually follows,
apparently has none.

27. This translation follows Legge, who, in turn, seems to follow the spirit of Zhu Xi's
commentary. An alternative translation would be "shelter them," but the sense of enabling
the people to become moral agents on their own fits in better with the last two lines of the
quotation.

28. Cf. *Mencius* 4B14.

29. See the *Analects* 8:18, 19.

the empire, it could not have been done without their fully devoting their minds to it, but they did not devote themselves to tilling the fields.

"I have heard of using Xia customs to transform the Yi,[30] but I have never heard of being transformed by the Yi. Chen Liang was a product of Chu. Delighting in the Way of the Duke of Zhou and Confucius, he came north to the central states to study it. Among those who studied in the north there was perhaps no one who surpassed him—he was what is called a valiant and distinguished scholar. You, Sir, and your brother, served him for several decades. But now that the teacher has died, you turn away from him.

"Formerly, when Confucius died, his disciples, after the three-year mourning period had passed, put their affairs in order and made ready to return home. On entering the presence of Zigong to take their leave of him, they looked at one another and wailed until they all lost their voices. Only then did they leave. Zigong returned, built himself a house on the site, and lived there alone for three more years.

"Another time Zixia, Zizhang, and Ziyou, believing that Youruo resembled the Sage, wished to serve him as they had served Confucius. They tried to persuade Zengzi to join them, but Zengzi said, 'It may not be. What has been washed in the waters of the Jiang and Han and bleached in the autumn sun—how glistening is its purity! Nothing can be added to it.' But now you turn your back on your teacher in order to become the disciple of this shrike-tongued barbarian from the south whose teachings are not those of the former kings. How different you are from Zengzi! I have heard of departing from a dark valley to repair to a tall tree; I have not heard of descending from a tall tree to enter a dark valley. In the 'Songs of Lu' it says:

The Rong and the Di he attacked,
And Jing and Shu he punished.[31]

---

30. In a later time this might be expressed as "using Chinese customs to transform barbarians," but in this context both the term "Chinese" and the term "barbarian" would be anachronistic.

31. Ode 300 (Legge, *Chinese Classics*, 4:620–30). The Rong and the Di were tribes to the west and the north, respectively. Jing refers to the area of the southern state of Chu and Shu to areas to the east of Chu. This poem is quoted again in 3B9.

"Whom the Duke of Zhou would attack, you would take as your teacher—certainly not a good change to make."

[Chen Xiang said,] "If Master Xu's Way were followed, there would not be two prices in the marketplace, nor would there be any duplicity in the state. If even a small boy were sent to the market, no one would deceive him. Equal lengths of cloth would be sold for a comparable price, as would equal weights of hemp and silk, and equal quantities of the five grains. This would be true as well of shoes of the same size."

Mencius said, "For things to be unequal is the natural tendency of things. Some are worth twice, some five times, or ten, or a hundred, or a thousand, or ten thousand times more than others. For the master to try to make them the same would bring chaos to the world. If fine shoes and poor shoes were priced the same, who would make fine shoes? To follow the way of Master Xu would be to lead people to practice duplicity. How could one govern a state this way?"

5] Yi Zhi, a Mohist, sought, through Xu Bi, to meet Mencius. Mencius said, "I certainly want to see him, but now I am still sick. When I have recovered from my illness, I will go myself to see him. Master Yi need not come here."

Another day Yi Zhi sought again to see Mencius. Mencius said, "Now I am able to see him. If I do not correct him, the Way will not be made apparent. I will correct him. I have heard that Master Yi is a Mohist. In regulating funeral practices, the Mohist way is that of simplicity, and Master Yi is contemplating changing the world accordingly. What makes him think that, unless the deceased are buried in this way, they are not honored? Master Yi himself buried his parents in a lavish style, thus serving his parents in a way that he himself disparages."

Master Xu informed Yi Zhi, who said, "According to the Confucian way, the ancients acted as if they were protecting an infant.[32] What does this teaching mean? To me it means that one should love without distinctions but that the love begins with parents and extends from there."

---

32. The line is apparently quoted from chap. 9 of the "Commentary" section of *The Great Learning*; see ibid., 2:370.

Master Xu told this to Mencius. Mencius replied, "Does Master Yi believe that a man's affection for his brother's child is just like his affection for the child of a neighbor? What he should have taken from the teaching [he cited] is that, if a child crawling toward a well is about to fall in, this is not the fault of the child. Heaven, in giving birth to living beings, causes them to have one root, while Master Yi supposes they have two roots.[33]

Now, in high antiquity there were some who did not bury their parents. When their parents died, they picked them up and cast them into a ditch. Another day, when they passed by, they saw that they were being devoured by foxes and wildcats and bitten by flies and gnats. Sweat broke out on their foreheads, and they averted their eyes to avoid the sight. The sweat was not because of what others would think but was an expression in their faces and eyes of what was present in their innermost hearts.[34] They returned home and brought earth-carrying baskets and spades to cover them over. Burying them was truly right, and filial children and benevolent people also act properly when they bury their parents."

Master Xu informed Master Yi of what Mencius had said. Master Yi reflected for a time and then said, "He has given me instruction."

33. David S. Nivison has written a revealing essay exploring the implications of this passage and this idea in particular ("Two Roots or One," in *The Ways of Confucianism: Investigations in Chinese Philosophy*, ed. Bryan W. Van Norden, 133–48 [La Salle, Ill.: Open Court, 1996]).

34. *Zhong xin* 中心, literally, "the middle heart," or what is in the very center of a person's being.

BOOK 3B

B1] Chen Dai said, "There is a certain smallness involved in not going to see the lords. If you were to go and see them now, your influence, if great, might cause one of them to become a king, and, even if it were small, it might cause one of them to become a hegemon. The *Record* speaks of 'bending the foot to straighten the yard.'[1] Surely this is worth trying?"

Mencius said, "Once when Duke Jing of Qi was hunting, he summoned his gamekeeper with a flag. The gamekeeper did not come, and the duke was about to have him killed. 'The dedicated officer does not forget that he may find himself in a ditch; the courageous officer does not forget that he may sacrifice his head.' What did Confucius find admirable in the gamekeeper's conduct? It was his refusal to go in response to an inappropriate summons.[2] What, then, about those who go without any summons at all? The saying about 'bending the foot in order to straighten the yard' has to do with profit, and if one is concerned with profit, wouldn't it also be possible to bend the yard in order to straighten the foot?

"Once Master Zhao Jian had Wang Liang serve as a charioteer for his favorite, Xi, but, in an entire day, they caught not a single bird. The favorite, Xi, returned and reported this, remarking that Wang Liang was 'the world's worst charioteer.' Someone reported this to Wang Liang, who said, 'I beg to be allowed to try again,' and, at his insistence, he was given permission. In a single morning they caught ten birds, whereupon the favorite, Xi, returned and reported that Liang was 'the world's

---

1. Actually, a *chi* 尺 is one Chinese foot, and a *xun* 尋 is eight feet. The *Record* referred to here has not been identified.

2. A similar version of this story, recalled in a different context, is found in 5B7.

best charioteer.' Master Jian said, 'I will make him drive your chariot,' but when he told Wang Liang, Wang Liang refused, saying, 'I drove for him according to the rules, and in an entire day he caught not a single bird. Then I drove for him in a cunning manner, and in a single morning he caught ten birds. The ode says,

> The driving was flawless
> The arrows shot forth like blows.[3]

I do not care to drive for a small person. I beg to be allowed to resign.'

"The charioteer was ashamed to be associated with the archer. Though, by being associated, they could have caught enough birds and animals to make a hill, he would not do it. If I were to bend the Way and follow them, what would I be? You, sir, are in error. No one has ever been able to straighten others by bending himself."

[3B2] Jing Chun said, "Truly, Gongsun Yan and Zhang Yi were great men, were they not? When they were angry, the lords would tremble in fear; when they dwelled in peace, the fires of conflict throughout the world were extinguished."

Mencius said, "How can they be considered great men? Have you, sir, not studied the *Book of Rituals*? When a man is capped, his father gives him orders. When a woman is married, her mother gives her orders, accompanying her to the door and cautioning her, 'You are going to your home. You must be reverent, you must be cautious. Do not disobey your husband.'[4] To consider compliance to be correct is the way of women.

"One who dwells in the wide house of the world, occupies his proper place in the world, and carries out the great Way of the world: when he is able to realize his intentions, carries them out for the sake of the people of the world, and when he cannot realize them, practices the Way alone. He cannot be led astray by riches and honor, moved by poverty and privation, or deflected by power or force. This is what I call a great man."

---

3. Ode 179 (Legge, *Chinese Classics*, 4:290).

4 Passages similar in content can be found in the *Book of Rituals* (*Yili* 儀禮).

33] Zhou Xiao[5] asked, "Did noble persons of antiquity serve in office?"

Mencius replied, "They did. The *Record* says, 'If Confucius went for three months without serving in office, he was disquieted. When he passed beyond the borders of a state, he always carried his gift of introduction.'[6] Gongming Yi said, 'Among the ancients, if someone went for three months without serving, people would offer their condolences.'"

"To offer condolences to someone who had gone for three months without serving—might this not suggest overzealousness?"

"For a man of service to lose his position is like one of the lords losing his state. It is said in the *Rites*, 'The lords plow and are assisted in plowing to produce millet. Their wives keep silkworms and make the silk for clothing. If the sacrificial animals are not perfect, the millet not pure, or the clothing not prepared, they do not dare to sacrifice. A man of service who has no field also does not sacrifice. If the sacrificial victims, the vessels, and the clothing are not prepared, they do not dare to sacrifice, nor do they feel at peace.[7] Is this not sufficient cause for condolences?"

"'When he passed beyond the borders of a state, he always carried his gift of introduction'—why was this?"

"Holding office for a man of service is like plowing for a farmer. When a farmer passes beyond the boundaries of a state, does he leave his plow behind?"

"The state of Jin[8] is also one that employs men of service, but I have never heard that the men of service were so zealous. If there is so much zealousness associated with serving, why do noble persons find it difficult to take office?"

"The birth of a son occasions the wish that he should have a wife; the birth of a daughter occasions the wish that she should have a marital

---

5. According to Zhao Qi, he was a native of Wei (or Liang); he apparently lived during the reigns of Kings Hui and Huai.

6. This refers to a gift that had the quality of a ritual object to be presented at an initial interview as a sign of one's sincerity. The text quoted is unknown.

7. Yang Bojun points out that there are parallels between what is contained in Mencius's discussion of sacrifices and material found in the "Jitung," "Quli," and "Wangzhi" chapters of the *Record of Rites* and the *Guliang zhuan*, Duke Huan, fourteenth year, though these texts, which were apparently compiled after the time of Mencius, are unlikely to be the source of his quotations (Yang Bojun, *Mengzi yizhu*).

8. Here referring to the state of Wei (or Liang).

home. As parents, all human beings have this mind. But if, without waiting for the command of parents or the permission of go-betweens, the young people bore holes in a wall in order to catch a glimpse of one another or scale the wall in order to come together, their parents and everyone in the state will hold them in low esteem. Men of antiquity always wanted to serve in office but were averse to doing so in a manner not consonant with the Way. To go forward in a manner not consonant with the Way is in a class with 'boring holes.'"

[3B4] Peng Geng[9] asked, "To go about followed by a train of several dozen carriages and a retinue of several hundred persons, feeding off of one lord after another in succession—is this not to be considered extravagant?"

Mencius said, "If it is not in accordance with the Way, one cannot receive from someone so much as a basket of rice. If it is in accordance with the Way, then receiving all-under-Heaven, as Shun did from Yao, is not to be considered extravagant. Do you, sir, feel it to be extravagant?"

"No. But it is inappropriate for a man of service who has not been given work to receive support."

"If you do not have circulation of products or exchange of services, allowing what one person has in excess to compensate for the deficiency of another, the farmers will have a surplus of grain and the women will have a surplus of cloth. If you have this circulation, then the artisans and carriage makers can all get their food from you. Here is a man who, at home, is filial and, in the outside world, deferential to elders. He holds to the Way of the former kings and waits for those who will study it in the future, yet you will not support him. Why is it that you will honor the woodworker and the carriage maker and disparage one who practices humaneness and rightness?"

"The intention of the woodworker and the carriage maker is to seek a living. According to the practice of the Way, is it also the motive of the noble person to seek a living?"

"What have you, sir, got to do with his motive? If someone does work for you, then you should feed him whenever you can. Do you reward the motive, or do you reward the work?"

---

9. According to Zhao Qi, he was a disciple of Mencius's.

"I reward the motive."

"Here is a man who destroys your tiles and smears paint on your walls. Since his motive is to seek a living, do you therefore reward him?"

"No."

"Then you do not reward motives. You reward work."

5] Wan Zhang[10] asked, "Song is a small state that is now on the point of practicing kingly government. If Qi and Chu despise and attack it, what is to be done?"

Mencius said, "When Tang dwelled in Bo, his territory was adjacent to Ge. The Lord of Ge was dissolute and did not perform sacrifices. Tang sent a messenger to inquire about this. He said, 'Why do you not perform sacrifices?' The Lord of Ge said, 'I have no way of obtaining sacrificial animals.' Tang had oxen and sheep sent to him. The Lord of Ge ate them and still he did not perform sacrifices. Tang again sent a messenger to inquire, 'Why do you not perform sacrifices?' The Lord of Ge replied, 'I have no way of obtaining millet.' Tang sent the people of Bo to help with the plowing and had the elderly and the young bring gifts of food. The Lord of Ge led his people out to intercept those who were bringing the wine and food, millet and rice, seizing the gifts and killing those who did not hand them over. There was a boy who was bearing provisions of millet and meat; he was killed and his present was seized. When the *Classic of Documents* says, 'The Lord of Ge was an enemy to the provision-bearers,'[11] it refers to this.

"It was because of the murder of this boy that Tang punished the Lord of Ge. All within the four seas said, 'It was not for the sake of all-under-Heaven but to avenge the loss of a common man and woman.'[12]

"When Tang began the work of punishment, he began with Ge.[13] In the course of eleven campaigns, he had no enemy under Heaven.

---

10. Wan Zhang has been considered to be Mencius's most outstanding disciple.

11. See "The Announcement of Zhong-hui," *Classic of Documents*, in Legge, *Chinese Classics*, 3:180.

12. That is, the parents of the murdered boy.

13. Probably quoting from a lost chapter of the *Classic of Documents*.

When he carried out the work of punishment in the east, the Yi in the west protested, and when he carried out the work of punishment in the south, the Di in the north protested, saying 'Why does he make us last?' The people looked forward to his coming as they did to rain in a time of great drought. Those who were going to market did not stop; those who were weeding in the fields did not cease working. While punishing their rulers, he consoled the people. He was like the falling of timely rain, and the people were greatly delighted. The *Classic of Documents* says, 'We await our ruler. When our ruler comes, there will be no more punishments.'[14]

"The state of You[15] would not be subjected to Zhou. King Wu punished them in the east. He brought tranquillity to their men and women. They filled baskets with black and yellow silk, requested an audience with our Zhou king, and became subjects of the great city of Zhou.[16] Gentlemen filled their baskets with black and yellow silks to welcome the gentlemen of Zhou. Common people brought baskets of food and vessels of drink to welcome the common people of Zhou. The king of Zhou saved the people from flood and fire and took captive only their oppressors.

"It says in the 'Great Declaration' [Taishi]:

Let our might be made manifest.
We will advance across the frontiers of You and seize its oppressive ruler.
Our punishments will be displayed.
We shall be more illustrious than Tang.[17]

---

14. "Taijia," part 2, *Classic of Documents*, in Legge, *Chinese Classics*, 3:208.

15. Commentators and translators disagree about the meaning of You 攸 in this context. I take You to be a feudal state in the east during the late Shang period. D. C. Lau also follows this interpretation (trans., *Mencius* [London: Penguin, 1970], 110). See also David S. Nivison, "On Translating Mencius," in *The Ways of Confucianism: Investigations in Chinese Philosophy*, ed. Bryan W. Van Norden (La Salle, Ill.: Open Court, 1996), 189–90.

16. The language of this passage is close to, though not identical with, language in the "Completion of the War" (Wu cheng) chapter of the *Classic of Documents*; see Legge, *Chinese Classics*, 3:313–14. My translation largely follows Yang Bojun. For a different interpretation, see Legge.

17. "The Great Declaration," part 2, *Classic of Documents*, in Legge, *Chinese Classics*, 3:293. The speaker here is King Wu, "the martial king" and founder of the Zhou dynasty.

Song is not, after all, practicing true kingly government. If it were practicing kingly government, everyone within the four seas would be raising their heads to watch for its ruler, wanting him to be their ruler, too. Great though Qi and Chu may be, what would there be to fear from them?"

6] Mencius said to Dai Busheng,[18] "You, sir, want your king to be good, do you not? Let me be clear in explaining this to you. Here is a high official from Chu who wishes his son to speak the language of Qi. Will he provide for him to be instructed by a man of Qi or by a man of Chu?"

"He will provide for a man of Qi to instruct him."

"But if there is one man of Qi instructing him and a whole crowd of Chu people clamoring all around him, then, although he may be beaten daily in an effort to get him to speak Qi, he will not be able to do so. And if he were placed in Zhuang or Yue[19] for several years, though he were beaten daily in an effort to get him to speak the language of Chu, he would also be unable to do so.

"In the belief that Xue Juzhou was a good man of service, you had him placed near the king. If, among those near the king, old and young, humble and exalted, all were Xue Juzhous, with whom would the king do anything that is not good? But if among those near him—old and young, humble and exalted—there is none that is a Xue Juzhou, with whom will the king do what is good? What can one Xue Juzhou alone do for the king of Song?"

7] Gongsun Chou asked, "What is righteous about not going to see the lords?"[20]

Mencius replied, "In ancient times, unless one had been a minister, one did not go to see the lord. Duan Ganmu[21] vaulted a wall in order to avoid meeting his lord. Xie Liu shut his door and would not allow the

18. Dai was a minister of the state of Song.

19. Commentators indicate that Zhuang was the name of a street in the Qi capital, while Yue was a neighborhood.

20. Compare with the question raised by Chen Dai at the opening of 3B1.

21. A worthy of the state of Wei, he lived in the time of Lord Wen (ca. 446–397 B.C.E.). His vaulting the wall was apparently intended to spare his lord from displaying excessive deference toward Duan.

lord inside. These two were overly scrupulous, however. If the situation is urgent, then one can see him.

"Yang Huo wanted to see Confucius, but he did not want to do so at the expense of ritual propriety. When a great officer sends a gift to a man of service and he is not at home to receive it, then he should go to the officer's gate and pay his respects. Yang Huo watched to see when Confucius was out and sent him a roasted pig. Confucius in turn watched to see when Yang Huo was out and went to pay his respects. On that occasion, since Yang Huo acted first, why should Confucius not have gone to see him?

"Zengzi said, 'Those who shrug their shoulders and laugh genially work harder than those who till the fields in summer.' Zilu said, 'Observe the flush of embarrassment in the face of one who pretends to agree with someone when he really does not. This is someone I do not care to know.' Looking at it from this perspective, one may know how the noble person cultivates himself."

[3B8] Dai Yingchi[22] said, "This year we are not able to adopt a tax of one part in ten and to abolish the duties charged at the borders and in the marketplaces. But tell me, please, what you think about my lightening the tax in the coming year and abolishing it thereafter?"

Mencius said, "Here is a man who each day steals one of his neighbor's chickens. Someone says to him, 'This is not the Way of a noble person.' He replies, 'If it please you, I shall cut back and steal only one chicken a month until next year, when I will stop.' If you know that this is not righteous, then just stop it. Why should you wait until next year?"

[3B9] Gongduzi said, "Outsiders all say that the Master is fond of argument. I venture to ask why?"

Mencius said, "How should I be fond of argument? I am compelled to do it. A long time has passed since the world came into being, and periods of order have alternated with periods of chaos. In the time of Yao, the waters overflowed their channels, inundating the Middle Kingdom; snakes and dragons dwelled in it, depriving the people of

22. A high officer of the state of Song.

a settled life. Those who lived in low-lying places made nests, while those who lived on higher ground made caves. The *Classic of Documents* says, 'The flood waters were a warning to us.'[23] 'The overflowing waters' refers to the waters of the deluge. Shun caused Yu to control them, and Yu dug out the earth so that the water would flow to the sea. He drove the snakes and dragons into the marshes. The waters flowed through the channels, and so it was with the Yangtze, the Huai, the Yellow, and the Han rivers. Once the dangers had been removed, and the birds and beasts that had injured people had disappeared, the people secured the level ground and could dwell upon it.

"Once Yao and Shun were no more, the Way of the sages declined, and oppressive rulers arose one after another. They destroyed houses and dwellings in order to make pools and ponds, and the people had no peaceful refuge. They caused fields to be abandoned to make parks and gardens, and the people could not get clothing and food. As deviant speech and oppressive actions became more prevalent, and as pools and ponds, thickets and marshes proliferated, wild animals returned. When it came down to the time of the tyrant *Zhou*, the world was once again in great chaos. The Duke of Zhou assisted King Wu and destroyed *Zhou*. He attacked Yan and, after three years, put its ruler to death. He drove Feilian[24] to a corner by the sea and annihilated him. The kingdoms he destroyed were fifty. He drove away tigers, leopards, rhinoceroses, and elephants, and the people of the world were greatly delighted. The *Classic of Documents* says,

> How great and splendid were the plans of King Wen,
> How greatly realized through the energies of King Wu!
> They are for the help and guidance of us, their descendants,
> Correct in everything, deficient in nothing.[25]

23. The phrase quoted by Mencius is a slight variant of a statement by the sage-king Shun in the "Counsels of the Great Yu" of the *Classic of Documents*. See Legge, *Chinese Classics*, 3:60.

24. Nefarious minister of the tyrant *Zhou*.

25. From the "Jun-ya" section of the *Classic of Documents*; translation adapted from Legge, *Chinese Classics*, 3:581.

"Again the world declined, and the Way was concealed. Deviant speech and oppressive actions again became prevalent. There were cases of ministers murdering their rulers and of sons murdering their parents. Confucius was afraid, and so wrote the *Spring and Autumn Annals*. The *Spring and Autumn Annals* are concerned with the affairs of the Son of Heaven, and thus Confucius said, 'It is by the *Spring and Autumn Annals* alone that I will be known, and for them alone that I will be condemned.'

"Once again sages and kings do not appear, the lords have become arbitrary and intemperate, and unemployed scholars indulge in uninhibited discussions. The words of Yang Zhu and Mo Di flow throughout the world; the teachings circulating in the world today all go back to Yang or Mo. Yang holds for egoism, which involves denial of one's sovereign; Mo holds for impartial care, which entails denial of one's parents.[26] To deny one's parents or to deny one's sovereign is to be an animal. Gongming Yi said, "In their kitchens there is fat meat. In their stables there are fat horses. And yet, the people have a lean and hungry look, and in the wilds there are those who have died of starvation. This is leading beasts to devour people."[27] If the ways of Yang and Mo are not stopped, and the way of Confucius is not made known, the people will be deceived by these deviant views, and the path of humaneness and rightness will be blocked. When the path of humaneness and rightness is blocked, animals are led to devour people, and people will be led to devour one another. I am fearful about this and defend the way of the former Sage by resisting Yang and Mo and banishing their licentious words. Those who espouse deviant views must be prevented from putting them into effect, for what is effected in the mind causes harm in affairs, and what is implemented in affairs causes harm to government. If a sage should arise again, he would not change my words.

---

26. The term translated as "impartial care" is *jian ai* 兼愛. I follow A. C. Graham's interpretation rather than rendering it as the more familiar "universal love." Graham argues that Mo Zi's *ai* suggests less warmth than the English word "love." *Jian* suggests "collaboration" and "inclusiveness" more than universality (*Disputers of the Tao* [La Salle, Ill.: Open Court, 1989], 41–43). See also 7A26 and 7B26.

27. See also 1A4, where Mencius himself makes this statement without attribution. For Gongming Yi, see 3A1.

"In former times Yu controlled the waters of the deluge, and the world was at peace. The Duke of Zhou controlled the Yi and the Di and drove away the wild animals, and the people enjoyed repose. Confucius wrote the *Spring and Autumn Annals*, and rebellious ministers and violent sons were struck with terror. The ode says,

The Rong and the Di he attacked,
And Jing and Shu he punished,
So that none of them will dare to withstand us.[28]

As the Duke of Zhou would have chastised those who denied fathers and rulers,[29] I, too, want to correct people's minds, to stop deviant speech, to resist perverse actions, to banish licentious words,[30] and so to carry on the work of the three Sages. In what way am I fond of argument? I am compelled to do it. Whoever can resist Yang and Mo with words is a follower of the Sage."

o] Kuang Zhang[31] said, "Surely Chen Zhongzi[32] must be acknowledged to be a man of integrity and purity? When he lived in Wuling, he went for three days without eating and could no longer hear or see. Over a well there was a plum tree, its fruit more than half eaten by worms. He crawled to it and ate some of the fruit, and after he had swallowed three bites, hearing was restored to his ears and sight to his eyes."

Mencius said, "Of the scholars of Qi, I must consider Zhongzi as the thumb among fingers, but how can he be considered pure? Only

28. Ode 300. Translation adapted from Legge, *Chinese Classics*, 4:626. See Mencius 3A4
29. Mencius likens the followers of Yang Zhu and Mo Zi to modern-day "barbarians."
30. Compare with what Mencius says in 2A2 about distorted, licentious, deviant, and evasive words.
31. A Qi general during the reigns of Kings Wei and Xuan.
32. Chen Zhongzi, also known as Tian Zhong, appears in several sources, including the "Nothing Indecorous" and "Contra Twelve Philosophers" chapters of the *Xunzi*. He was a relative of the king of Qi and apparently a follower of Xu Xing. As Kuang Zhang's comment suggests, Chen had a reputation for integrity and purity, insisting on growing all his own food and refusing to attend at the courts of rulers he considered corrupt. Mencius seems to have found his fixation on personal purity excessive and perhaps even hypocritical. See also 7A34.

after having become an earthworm, which eats the dry earth above and drinks from the Yellow Springs below, could one begin to fulfill Zhongzi's principles. Did a Boyi or a Robber Zhi build the house where Zhongzi dwells? Did a Boyi or a Robber Zhi plant the millet he eats? These are things we cannot know."

"Of what consequence is this? He himself weaves sandals, and his wife spins hempen thread to exchange."

"Zhongzi is from a prominent family of Qi. His older brother, Dai, received from Ge a stipend of ten thousand *zhong*, but he considered his brother's emolument to be an unrighteous emolument and would not eat from it. He considered his brother's house to be an unrighteous house and would not live in it. Shunning his brother and parting from his mother, he went to live in Wuling. One day when he returned, someone gave his brother a live goose. Frowning, he said, 'What will you use that cackler for?' The next day his mother killed the goose and gave it to him to eat. When his brother came in from outside and said, 'This is the meat of that cackler,' he went out and threw it up. What his mother gave him he would not eat, while what his wife gave him he would eat. He would not live in his brother's house, but he would live in Wuling. Can this be considered fulfilling his principles in a consistent manner? Only if one were to become an earthworm could one begin to fulfill such principles as Zhongzi holds."

BOOK 4A

1] Mencius said, "If one had the eyesight of Li Lou[1] and the dexterity of Master Gongshu[2] but lacked the compass and square, one would not be able to form squares and circles. If one had the keen ear of Music Master Kuang[3] but lacked the six pitch pipes, one would not be able to adjust the five notes correctly. If one had the Way of Yao and Shun but lacked humane government, one would not be able to rule the world. Though he may have a humane heart and a reputation for humaneness, one from whom the people receive no benefits will not serve as a model for later generations because he does not practice the Way of the former kings. Therefore it is said,

> Goodness alone does not suffice for the conduct of government;
> Laws alone do not implement themselves.

The ode says,

> Not transgressing, not forgetting,
> But following the statutes of old.[4]

No one has ever erred by following the laws of the former kings.

1. According to tradition, he lived at the time of the Yellow Emperor and was gifted with unusual visual acuity, so that he could see something as small as "the tip of an autumn hair."
2. A native of the state of Lu, he lived between the time of Confucius and Mo Zi and was famous as a gifted artisan.
3. Music master to Duke Ping of Jin, he became the most famous music master in the history of ancient China.
4. Ode 249 (Legge, *Chinese Classics*, 4:481–83).

"The sages, having fully utilized the strength of their eyes, extended it through the compass, square, level, and plumb line, which have unlimited power to make things square, round, level, and straight. Having fully utilized the power of their ears, they extended it through the six pitch pipes, which have unlimited power to correct the five notes. And when they had fully utilized the thoughts of their hearts, they extended it through a government that could not bear to see the sufferings of others, and their benevolence spread to all-under-Heaven. Therefore it is said, 'To build high, one should start from the height of a hill; to dig deep, one should start from the depths of a streambed. And when it comes to government, can anyone be considered wise who does not follow the Way of the former kings?

"Therefore only the humane should be in high positions. When one lacking in humaneness occupies a high position, his wickedness spreads to everyone. When, above, the Way is not considered, then, below, the laws are not preserved; when courtiers do not believe in the Way, artisans do not believe in measures; when gentlemen offend against rightness, small people offend against the criminal laws. It is a matter of sheer good fortune if the state survives. Therefore it is said, 'When the city walls are not complete or arms abundant, this is not a calamity for the state. When fields and wilds have not been opened up to cultivation or goods amassed, this is not a threat to the state. But when, above, there is an absence of ritual propriety and, below, an absence of learning, rebels will rise up and the state will soon perish.'

"The ode says,

When Heaven is about to move,
Do not be so talkative.[5]

"To be talkative is to be negligent. Serving the ruler without rightness, advancing and withdrawing without regard to ritual propriety, and maligning the Way through one's words—this is like being negligent. Therefore it is said, 'Charging one's ruler with what is difficult is called showing respect for him. Urging goodness while warning against

5. Ode 254 (ibid., 4:499–504).

evil is called being reverent toward him. Saying that he is "unable to do it" is called injuring him.' "[6]

A2] Mencius said, "From the compass and the square comes the ultimate standard for circles and squares, and from the sage comes the ultimate standard in human relations.

"One who desires to be a ruler must fully develop the Way of the ruler; one who desires to be a minister must fully develop the Way of the minister. In either case, all that is required is to take Yao and Shun as the model. Not to serve one's ruler as Shun served Yao is not to respect one's ruler; not to rule the people as Yao ruled them is to act as a plunderer of the people. Confucius said, 'There are just two ways: being humane and being inhumane.' One whose oppression of his people is extreme will himself be killed and his state will be lost. One who is less extreme will place himself in danger and weaken his state. He will be called 'the Dark' or 'the Tyrannical,'[7] and though he may have filial sons and devoted grandsons, they will be unable in a hundred generations to change those names.

"The ode says,

The mirror of the Yin is not far off,
It is found in the time of the last of the Xia.[8]

This is what was meant."

A3] Mencius said, "The way the three dynasties gained the empire was through humaneness, and the way they lost it was through not being humane. So it is too in the flourishing or decline of states, and in their preservation or loss. If the Son of Heaven is not humane, he will be unable to protect all within the four seas. If a feudal lord is not humane,

---

6. See 1A7, where Mencius makes the distinction between "not doing" something and "being unable" to do it. See also 2A6.

7. The names of two rulers of ill repute in the Zhou; they are mentioned again in 6A6.

8. Ode 255, which suggests that the experience of the tyrant Jie, the last ruler of the Xia dynasty, should be taken as an example by later rulers. The Xia (1907?–1555? B.C.E.) was supposed to have been the first dynasty that, in its decadence, succumbed to attack by the Shang.

he will be unable to protect the altars of the soil and grain. If a high officer is not humane, he will be unable to protect the ancestral temple. And if an ordinary person is not humane, he will be unable to protect his four limbs. Now, to dislike death and ruin and yet to take pleasure in not being humane is like disliking drunkenness and yet forcing oneself to drink to excess."

[4A4] Mencius said, "If one loves others and yet they show no affection in return, he should turn within and examine his own humaneness; if one rules others and yet they are not well governed, he should examine his own wisdom; if one behaves with propriety toward others yet they do not respond appropriately, he should examine his own reverence. Whenever one acts to no avail, one should turn within and examine oneself. When one has made one's own person correct, the rest of the world will follow. The ode says,

> Long may you be worthy of the Mandate,
> And seek for yourself many blessings."[9]

[4A5] Mencius said, "Among the people there is the common saying, 'The empire, the state, the family.' The empire has its basis in the state; the state has its basis in the family, and the family has its basis in oneself."[10]

[4A6] Mencius said, "Governing is not difficult. It consists in not offending the great families. What the great families admire will be admired by the entire state. What the entire state admires will be admired throughout the world. Thus Virtuous teaching surges floodlike to all within the four seas."

[4A7] Mencius said, "When the Way prevails in the world, those of small Virtue serve those of great Virtue and those of lesser ability serve those of greater ability. When the Way does not prevail in the world, the small serve the great, and the weak serve the strong. Both of these are ow-

---

9. Ode 235 (Legge, *Chinese Classics*, 4:427–31).
10. Compare the similar idea in section 4 of *The Great Learning*.

ing to Heaven. Those who follow Heaven are preserved, while those who rebel against Heaven perish. Duke Jing of Qi said, 'To be unable to command others and unwilling to receive their orders is to be destined for destruction.' With flowing tears he gave his daughter to Wu in marriage.[11]

"Now the small states model themselves on the great states and yet are ashamed to receive their orders. This is like a disciple being ashamed to receive commands from his teacher. For one who feels thus ashamed, there could be no better course than to take King Wen as his teacher. With King Wen as a model, he will, in five years, if his state is large, or in seven years, if his state is small, be sure to govern all-under-Heaven. The ode says,

> The descendants of Shang,
> Numbered more than hundreds of thousands,
> But when the Mandate came from the Lord-on-High,
> The lords submitted to Zhou.
> The lords submitted to Zhou,
> The Mandate of Heaven is not constant.
> The officers of Yin, admirable and earnest,
> Pour out libations at our capital.[12]

"Confucius said, 'Against such humaneness, they could not be considered a multitude.' If the lord of a state loves humaneness, he will have no enemy in the world. But to wish to have no enemy in the world without using humaneness is like grabbing hold of something hot without first cooling it off with water. The ode says,

> Who can grab hold of something hot,
> Without first cooling it with water?"[13]

---

11. Not to King Wu of Zhou (whose name is written with a different character) but to the ruler of the state of Wu, still considered only minimally civilized. The duke's daughter suffered an early death, ostensibly of grief.

12. Ode 235 (Legge, *Chinese Classics*, 4:427–31).

13. Ode 257 (Legge, *Chinese Classics*, 4:519–27).

[4A8] Mencius said, "Is it possible to speak with those who are not humane? Mistaking danger for peace and calamity for profit, they take pleasure in what occasions their ruin. If, despite their inhumanity, it were possible to talk with them, would we have this ruin of states and this destruction of families?

"There was a boy who was singing,

When the waters of the Cang-lang are clear,
I can wash my cap strings.
When the waters of the Cang-lang are muddy,
I can wash my feet.

"Confucius said, 'Listen to him, my little ones. When it is clear, it washes cap strings; when it is muddy, it washes the feet. This is all determined by the water itself.' A man must demean himself; only then will others demean him. A family must destroy itself; only then will others destroy it. A state must attack itself and only then will others attack it. This is what is meant when the "Taijia" says,

When Heaven makes misfortunes,
It is still possible to escape them.
When the misfortunes are of our own making,
It is no longer possible to live."[14]

[4A9] Mencius said, "Jie and *Zhou* lost the world because they lost the people, and they lost the people because they lost the hearts of the people. There is a Way to obtain the world: one gains the world by gaining the people; when one gains the people, one gains the world. There is a Way of gaining the people: by gaining their hearts one gains the people. There is a Way to gain their hearts: gather for them the things

---

14. See the "Taijia" section of the *Classic of Documents*, in Legge, *Chinese Classics*, 3:207. This passage is also quoted in 2A4.

that you desire; do not impose on them the things that you dislike.[15] The people's turning to humaneness is like water flowing downward or wild animals heading for the wilds. Thus, as the otter drives the fish toward the deep and the sparrow hawk drives the smaller birds toward the thicket, Jie and *Zhou* drove the people toward Tang and Wu. If, in the world today, there were a ruler who loved humaneness, the lords would all drive the people to him, and, though he might wish not to become a king, he could not help but do so.

"Those in the world today who wish to become a true king are like the case of needing to find an herb[16] requiring three years of drying and preparation to treat an illness of seven years' duration. If it has not been stored up, to the end of his life, the patient will never have an adequate supply. If rulers do not commit themselves to humaneness, they will endure a lifetime of grief and disgrace and finally sink into death and destruction.

"This is what is meant when the ode says,

How can they become good?
They only lead one another toward drowning."[17]

10] Mencius said, "With those who do violence to themselves, one cannot speak, nor can one interact with those who throw themselves away. To deny propriety and rightness in one's speech is what is called 'doing violence to oneself.' To say, 'I am unable to abide in humaneness or to follow rightness' is what is called 'throwing oneself away.' For human beings, humaneness is the peaceful dwelling, and rightness is the correct path. To abandon the peaceful dwelling and not abide in it and to reject the right road and not follow it—how lamentable!"

15. This translation—which assumes reciprocity between the ruler and his subjects—is unusual. As Nivison has observed, Dobson is virtually alone in interpreting this to mean that the ruler judges what the people desire based on his own desires and what they dislike based on his own antipathies. See David S. Nivison, "On Translating Mencius," in *The Ways of Confucianism: Investigations in Chinese Philosophy*, ed. Bryan W. Van Norden (La Salle, Ill.: Open Court, 1996), 198.

16. The *ai* 艾, or artemisia plant, used in moxibustion.

17. Ode 257 (Legge, *Chinese Classics*, 4:519–27).

[4A11] Mencius said, "The Way lies in what is near yet is sought in what is far off. Our work lies in what is easy yet is sought in what is difficult. If all people would love their parents and be respectful to their elders, the whole world would be at peace."

[4A12] Mencius said, "When those occupying positions below do not gain the confidence of those above, they cannot succeed in governing the people. There is a way to gain the confidence of those above: one who does not inspire the trust of friends will not have the confidence of those above. There is a way to gain the trust of friends: one who does not serve his parents so as to please them will not inspire the trust of friends. There is a way to please one's parents: one who turns within and finds himself not to be sincere does not please his parents. There is a way to be sincere within oneself: if one is not clear about what is good, one will not be sincere within oneself. Therefore, to be sincere is the Way of Heaven, and to think about sincerity is the human Way. It has never happened that one who is sincere fails to move others, or that one who is not sincere is able to move others."[18]

[4A13] Mencius said, "Boyi,[19] having fled from *Zhou*, was living by the shore of the northern sea. Hearing of the rise of King Wen, he bestirred himself and said, 'Would it not be best to go back and follow him? I have heard that Xibo is good at caring for the old.' Taigong,[20] having fled from *Zhou*, was living by the shore of the eastern sea. Hearing of the rise of King Wen, he bestirred himself and said, 'Would it not be best to go back and follow him? I have heard that Xibo is good at caring for the old.'[21]

"These two were the world's greatest elders, and their following King Wen meant that the fathers of the world were following him. When the

---

18. Compare 4A4 and the *Doctrine of the Mean*, chap. 20.

19. Boyi and his younger brother, Shuqi, both left their ancestral home and adopted a kind of exile because neither was willing to succeed their father at the expense of the other.

20. Taigong was the epithet of Lu Shang, who became one of the advisers to Kings Wen and Wu of Zhou. King Wen told Lu Shang that "my grandfather looked for you long ago," from which came the name Taigong Wang, or, in Legge's translation, "Grandfather's Hope" (Legge, *Chinese Classics*, 2:303).

21. This account is repeated in 7A22.

fathers of the world followed him, where else could the sons go? If any of the lords practiced the government of King Wen, within seven years, he would assuredly be governing the world."

14] Mencius said, "When Ran Qiu served as chief officer of the Ji clan, he was unable to improve the quality of their Virtue, and yet he doubled the tax in grain over what the people had previously paid. Confucius said, 'Qiu is no follower of mine. Little ones, you may beat the drums and attack him.'[22]

"From this it can be seen that one who enriched a ruler who was not given to the practice of humane government was cast off by Confucius. How much more would this be true in the case of one bent on making war? Wars that arise from territorial contests kill so many people that the fields are packed with corpses; wars that arise from contests over cities kill so many people that the cities are packed with corpses. This is what is called leading the earth to devour human flesh. Death is not an adequate punishment for such a crime. Therefore, those who are skilled in war should suffer the highest punishment, followed by those who are responsible for bringing about alliances among the feudal lords, and then by those who open up uncultivated lands and oblige the people to cultivate them."

15] Mencius said, "When observing someone there is nothing more telling than the pupil of the eye. In the pupil one's wickedness cannot be concealed. When one is correct within one's innermost being, the pupil will be clear. When one is not correct within one's innermost being, the pupil will be dull. If one listens to his words and observes the pupils of his eyes, what can a person hide?"

16] Mencius said, "One who is respectful is not contemptuous of other people, and one who is frugal does not extort from others. A ruler who is contemptuous of others and extorts from them is only afraid that they will not obey him. How can they be respectful and frugal? How can respect and frugality be expressed through a pleasing voice and an ingratiating manner?"

22. *Analects* 11:16.

[4A17] Chunyu Kun[23] said, "Is it a matter of ritual propriety that, in giving and receiving things, men and women should not touch one another?"[24]

Mencius said, "This is according to ritual."

"If one's sister-in-law is drowning, may one save her with his hand?"

"If one's sister-in-law were drowning and one did not save her, one would be a wolf. For men and women, in giving and receiving, not to touch one another is according to ritual. To save a sister-in-law from drowning by using one's hand is a matter of expedience."

"Now the whole world is drowning, and yet you do not save it. Why is this?"

"When the world is drowning, one saves it through the Way. If one's sister-in-law is drowning, one saves her with one's hand. Would you like me to save the world with my hand?"

[4A18] Gongsun Chou said, "Why is it that a gentleman does not instruct his own son?"

Mencius said, "The circumstances do not allow it. Instruction necessarily involves correction, and when the correction is not effective, the next thing is that they become angry. When they become angry, then, paradoxically, they hurt one another. The son says, 'My master instructs me in what is correct, but my master himself does not display correct behavior.' This is when father and son hurt one another, and for a father and son to hurt one another is a terrible thing.

"In ancient times people exchanged sons and taught one another's sons. Between fathers and sons there should be no carping about goodness, because when there is carping about goodness, there is disaffection, and nothing could be more unfortunate than disaffection."

[4A19] Mencius said, "Of all forms of service, which is the greatest? It is serving one's parents. Of all kinds of vigilance, which is the greatest? It is

23. A man of Qi who attended at the courts of King Wei of Qi and King Xuan of Qi and also at the court of King Hui of Liang.

24. The prohibition Chunyu Kun invokes here is found in the "Chu Li" chapter of the *Book of Rites*.

vigilance over one's own person. I have heard of those who, not losing control of themselves, have been able to serve their parents, but I have never heard of those who, having lost control of themselves, have been able to serve their parents. There are many services one must perform, but the serving of one's parents is the root of all of them. There are many kinds of vigilance that one must exercise, but vigilance over one's own person is the root of all of them.

"When Master Zeng was nurturing Zeng Xi, he always provided wine and meat, and when the meal was being cleared, he always asked to whom the remaining food should be given. If his father asked whether there was food remaining, he always replied that there was. When Zeng Xi died, and Zeng Yuan was nurturing Master Zeng, he always provided wine and meat, but when the meal was being cleared, he did not ask to whom the remaining food should be given, and if his father asked if there was food remaining, he said that it had been finished, because he intended to serve it again. This is what is called 'nourishing the mouth and body,' whereas doing it in the way Master Zeng did can be called 'nourishing the intentions.' In serving one's parents, the way Master Zeng did it is correct."

o] Mencius said, "It is not enough to censure a ruler over those who have been appointed to office, nor is it enough to criticize the policies of his government. Only a great man can correct what is wrong in a ruler's mind. If the ruler is humane, everyone will be humane. If the ruler does what is right, everyone will do what is right. If the ruler is correct, everyone will be correct. Once the ruler has been rectified, the state will be settled."

ɪ] Mencius said, "There have been cases of unanticipated praise and also of unexpectedly overexacting criticism."

ɪ2] Mencius said, "A person who makes light with his words is not qualified to assume responsibility."

ɪ3] Mencius said, "The trouble with people lies in their desire to be the teachers of others."

[4A24]   Master Yuezheng[25] went to Qi in the retinue of Ziao[26] and went to see Mencius. Mencius said, "Did you, sir, also come to see me?"

"Master, why do you speak such words?"

Mencius said, "How many days has it been since you came here?"

"[I arrived] yesterday."

"Yesterday! Then is it not right that I speak these words?"

"My lodging had not yet been arranged."

"Have you heard that one's lodging must be arranged before one seeks to see his elder?"

"I am at fault."

[4A25]   Mencius said to Master Yuezheng, "Your having come here in the retinue of Ziao was only because of the food and drink. I would not have thought that you, given your study of the Way of the ancients, would have done this for food and drink."

[4A26]   Mencius said, "There are three things that are unfilial, and the greatest of them is to have no posterity.[27] Shun married without informing his parents out of concern that he might have no posterity. The noble person considers that it was as if he had informed them."

[4A27]   Mencius said, "The most authentic expression of humaneness is serving one's parents; the most authentic expression of rightness is following one's older brother; the most authentic expression of wisdom is knowing these two things and not departing from them; the most authentic expression of ritual propriety is regulating and adorning these two; the most authentic expression of music is in taking joy in these two. When there is joy, they grow; when they grow, how can they be stopped? When they come to the point where they cannot be stopped, then, without realizing it, one's feet begin to step in time to them and one's hands begin to dance them out."

25. Yuezheng Ko. See 1B16, 6B13, and 7B25.

26. Wang Huan. See 4B27.

27. According to Zhao Qi, the other two expressions of unfiliality were acquiescing in a lack of rightness on the part of a parent and failing to provide for them in their old age.

8]   Mencius said, "Greatly contented, the whole world turned to him, yet he regarded the whole world turning to him, greatly contented, as like so much grass. Only Shun was like this. He thought that if he could not win the hearts of his parents, he could not be a human being, and that if he could not reach an accord with his parents, he could not be a son. Through Shun's fulfilling the Way of serving his parents, Gusou[28] came to be pleased, and when Gusou came to be pleased, the world was transformed. When Gusou came to be pleased, all the fathers and sons in the world became secure. This is called 'great filiality.'"

28. Gusou was Shun's father. His name literally means "the blind man," and he is depicted as morally as well as physically blind. He first appears in the literature in the "Canon of Yao" in the *Classic of Documents*. See Legge, *Chinese Classics*, 3:26; and also 5A2 and 5A4.

BOOK 4B

[4B1] Mencius said, "Shun was born in Zhufeng, moved to Fuxia, and died in Mingtiao—a man of the Eastern Yi. King Wen was born at Mount Qi, in Zhou, and died at Biying—a man of the Western Yi. In terms of place, they were separated from one another by more than a thousand *li*, and in terms of time, by more than a thousand years. But when they realized their intentions and implemented them in the Middle Kingdom, it was like uniting the two halves of a tally: the sage who came earlier and the sage who came later were one in their dispositions."

[4B2] Zichan,[1] when he was in charge of the government of Zheng, used his own carriage to convey people across the Chen and Wei rivers. Mencius said, "He was kind, but he did not understand the practice of government. When the footbridges are completed in the eleventh month and the carriage bridges in the twelfth month of each year,[2] the people will not have the difficulty of having to wade across. The gentleman should practice government equitably. When he travels, he may have people cleared from his path. How can he convey each person across the river? If one who governs tries to please each person, the day will not be sufficient for him to do his work."

[4B3] Mencius said to King Xuan of Qi, "When the ruler regards his ministers as his hands and feet, the ministers regard the ruler as their stomachs and hearts. When the ruler regards his ministers as dogs and horses, the ministers regard the ruler as just another person. When the ruler

---

1. Gongsun Qiao (d. 522 B.C.E.) was prime minister of Zheng.
2. This corresponds to the ninth and tenth months of the present lunar calendar.

regards his ministers as dirt and grass, the ministers regard the ruler as a bandit and an enemy."

The king said, "According to ritual, a minister wears mourning for a ruler he has once served. How must one behave in order for this practice to be followed?"

Mencius said, "When a minister whose admonitions have been followed and whose advice has been heeded, with the result that benefits have extended down to the common people, has reason to depart the state, the ruler sends an escort to conduct him beyond its borders. He also prepares the way for him at his destination. Only after he has been gone for three years without returning does the ruler repossess his land and residence. This is called the threefold courtesy. When a ruler acts in such a way, the minister will wear mourning for him. Now, however, a minister's admonitions are not followed and his advice is not heeded, with the result that benefits do not extend down to the common people. When he has reason to depart, the ruler tries to seize and detain him and even tries to place him in extreme jeopardy at his destination. He repossesses his land and residence on the day of his departure. This is known as being a bandit and an enemy. What mourning should there be for a bandit and an enemy?"

B4] Mencius said, "When the scholars are put to death though they are guilty of no crime, the great officers may leave; when the people are slaughtered though they are guilty of no crime, the scholars may depart."

B5] Mencius said, "If the ruler is humane, everyone will be humane. If the ruler keeps to rightness, everyone will keep to rightness."

B6] Mencius said, "A ritual that is not a true ritual, rightness that is not truly right—the great person does not practice them."

B7] Mencius said, "Those who keep to the Mean nurture those who do not; those with talent nurture those who lack it. Therefore people take pleasure in having exemplary fathers and older brothers. If those who keep to the Mean were to cast aside those who do not, and if those with talent were to cast aside those who lack it, then the space between the exemplary and those found wanting would narrow to less than an inch."³

[4B8] Mencius said, "Only when a person has some actions that he will not take is he able to take action."

[4B9] Mencius said, "Before speaking of what is not good in others one should consider what calamities may ensue."

[4B10] Mencius said, "Confucius did nothing excessive."

[4B11] Mencius said, "The great man does not think about whether his words will be credible or his actions effective. He thinks merely about whether they will embody rightness."

[4B12] Mencius said, "The great person is one who does not lose the child's mind."

[4B13] Mencius said, "Caring for one's parents while they are alive cannot be considered a great thing. It is only through performing the rituals that honor them appropriately in death that one does the great thing."

[4B14] Mencius said, "The noble person delves into it deeply according to the Way, wishing to get it in himself. As he gets it in himself, he abides in it calmly; abiding in it calmly, he trusts in it deeply; trusting in it deeply, he draws on its source, which he finds both to his left and to his right. This is why the noble person wishes to get it for himself."

[4B15] Mencius said, "After extensive learning and thorough discussion, one should go back and express it with concision."

[4B16] Mencius said, "One who would use goodness to cause people to submit has never been able to cause their submission. Let him, through goodness, nurture people, and then he will be able to effect the submission

---

3. See the *Doctrine of the Mean*, chap. 4.

of the whole world. It has never happened that one to whom the people of the world have not yet submitted in their hearts has become a true king."

7] Mencius said, "Words that do not correspond to reality are unfortunate, and what is really most unfortunate is to obscure the reputation of a person of ability."

8] Xuzi said, "Confucius often praised water, saying, 'Ah, Water! Water!' What was it that he found in water?"

Mencius said, "A spring of water gushing forth rests neither day nor night. It fills the hollows and then moves on to reach the four seas. What has a source is like this, and this is what he found worthy of praise. If there is no source, then in the seventh and eighth months, when the rain falls copiously, the channels in the fields are all filled, yet one may expect that they will soon be dried up again. Therefore, the noble person is ashamed to have a reputation that exceeds actuality."

9] Mencius said, "That wherein human beings differ from the birds and beasts is but slight. The majority of people relinquish this, while the noble person retains it. Shun was clear about the multitude of things and observant of human relationships. Humaneness and rightness were the source of his actions; he did not just perform acts of humaneness and rightness."

10] Mencius said, "Yu disliked fine wine but loved good words. Tang held fast to the Mean[4] and appointed persons according to their ability rather than adhering to fixed criteria. King Wen looked on the people as he would on a person who was injured and aspired toward the Way though he could not see it realized.[5] King Wu did not slight those who were near, nor did he forget those who were distant. The Duke of

---

4. The injunction to "hold fast to the Mean" is found in "The Counsels of the Great Yu," in the *Classic of Documents*. See Legge, *Chinese Classics*, 3:61–62.

5. This was left to King Wu, who succeeded him and completed the conquest of the Shang.

Zhou thought of bringing [the virtues of] those three kings[6] together in himself and demonstrating the four kinds of service that they performed.[7] When he found any practice in his own time that did not conform with theirs, he looked up and thought about it from day until night. When he was fortunate enough to get it, he sat and waited for the dawn."

[4B21] Mencius said, "With the disappearance of the wooden-clappered bell of the kings,[8] the odes ceased, and only then were the *Spring and Autumn Annals* made. The *Annals of Jin*, the *Taowu of Chu*, and the *Spring and Autumn of Lu* are alike in dealing with persons such as Duke Huan of Qi and Duke Wen of Jin and being written in a historical style. Confucius said, 'The moral significance of the *Spring and Autumn Annals*—I venture to say I understand it.'"

[4B22] Mencius said, "The influence of a noble person ends with the fifth generation, and the influence of a lesser person also ends with the fifth generation. Although I was not able to be a follower of Confucius, I have cultivated myself through others."

[4B23] Mencius said, "When it is permissible to accept but also not to accept, then accepting involves an injury to scrupulousness. When it is permissible to give but also not to give, then giving involves an injury to kindness. When it is permissible to die but also not to die, then dying involves an injury to courage."

[4B24] Peng Meng learned archery from Yi. When he had fully mastered Yi's Way, he thought that the only one in the world superior to himself was Yi. So he killed Yi.

---

6. That is, Yu was regarded as the founder of the Xia dynasty and Tang as the founder of the Shang. Wen and Wu are often taken together, as here, almost as one composite dynastic founder of the Zhou.

7. That is, as recounted in the preceding descriptions of these kings.

8. The translation is based on the textual variant described by Yang Bojun in his note on this section in his *Mengzi yizhu* (see 3B3, n. 7). What is referred to here is the ancient practice of kings' sending out heralds with wooden-clappered bells to collect odes or songs from among the people. The suggestion is not that the existing odes were lost but that new odes were no longer made.

Mencius said, "Yi, too, was culpable in this."

Gongming Yi[9] said, "He seems to have been without culpability."

[Mencius replied,] "It may have been small, but how can it be said that he was without culpability?" The people of Zheng sent Zizhuo Ruzi to invade Wei. Wei sent Yugong Si in pursuit of him. Zizhuo Ruzi said, 'Today I am sick and cannot hold my bow. I shall die.' He asked his driver, 'Who is it that is pursuing me?' The driver said, 'Yugong Si.' Zizhuo Ruzi said, 'I shall live.' The driver said, 'Yugong Si is the best archer in Wei. And yet you say, "I shall live." What do you mean?' He said, 'Yugong Si learned archery from Yingong To, and Yingong To learned archery from me. Yingong To is a principled person and the friends whom he chooses must be principled as well.' When Yugong Si caught up, he said, 'Master, why are you not holding your bow?' Zizhuo Ruzi said, 'Today I am sick and cannot hold my bow.' Yugong Si said, 'I learned archery from Yingong To, and Yingong To learned it from you, Master. I cannot bear to inflict harm on you by using your Way against you. Still, today's work is the work of the ruler, which I do not dare to neglect.' He drew out his arrows, knocked the tips off against the wheel, and shot off four of them before returning."

25]   Mencius said, "If Lady Xi[10] had been covered in filth, people would all have held their noses as they passed her. But, although a person is ugly, it is possible, through fasting and purification, to become fit to perform sacrifices to the Lord-on-High."[11]

26]   Mencius said, "Those in the world who speak about human nature only consider its original state and take its original state to be fundamentally self-interested. What I dislike in the wise is their habit of boring their way through. If the wise resembled Yu in his directing the flow of the waters, there would be nothing to dislike in their wisdom. The way Yu directed the waters was by directing them in a way that was unforced. If the wise would also direct their thoughts in a way that was unforced, then their wisdom would also be great indeed.

9. See 3A1 and 3B3, 9.
10. A legendary beauty.
11. That is, the supreme spirit Shang-ti.

"Heaven is high and the stars are far away. Yet if we seek out how they were formerly, we may calculate a solstice of a thousand years from now without rising from our seats."[12]

[4B27] Master Gonghang lost a son, and the *youshi* Wang Huan[13] went to offer his condolences. When he entered, some people came over to speak with him and others came to speak with him as he assumed the place of the *youshi*. Mencius did not speak with him, and the *youshi* was not pleased. "All the gentlemen spoke with me" he said. "Mencius alone did not. He treated me disrespectfully.'

When Mencius heard of this he said, "According to ritual, when one is at court, one should not step across the seats in order to talk with others, nor should one step across steps in order to bow to them. I wished to observe the rites, but Ziao thought I was being disrespectful. Isn't this quite strange?"

[4B28] Mencius said, "That whereby the noble person differs from others is that he preserves his mind. The noble person preserves his mind through humaneness, preserves his mind through courtesy. One who is humane loves other people; one who possesses courtesy respects other people. One who loves others always is loved by them; one who respects others is always respected by them.

"Here is a man who treats me with malice. [Receiving such treatment,] the noble person must turn within: 'I must not have been humane; I must have been lacking in courtesy, or how could such a thing have happened to me?' If, on turning within, one finds oneself to be humane, if on turning within one finds oneself to be courteous and yet the maliciousness continues, the noble person must *again* turn within: 'I must not have shown good faith.' If, on turning within, one finds good

---

12. The interpretation of this passage is based on the analysis of A. C. Graham. See his "The Background of the Mencian (Mengzian) Theory of Human Nature," and my "Mengzian Arguments on Human Nature (Ren Xing)," both in *Essays on the Moral Philosophy of Mengzi*, ed. Xiusheng Liu and Philip J. Ivanhoe, 1–63 and 64–100, respectively (Indianapolis: Hackett, 2002).

13. Also known as Ziao, he appears briefly in 4A24 and 4A25. What his official position of *youshi* 右師 entailed in the fourth-century context is unclear.

faith in oneself and still the maliciousness continues, the noble person will say, 'This is a wild man. Since he is like this, how then can one choose between him and the animals? Why should I contend with an animal?' Therefore the noble person has anxiety that lasts a lifetime rather than troubles that occupy a morning. And indeed the anxiety has a cause: 'Shun was a human being; I, too, am a human being. Shun was a model for the world, one that could be transmitted to later generations. If I am nothing more than a villager, this is something to be anxious about.' And what kind of anxiety is it? Simply to be like Shun; that is all. There is nothing that troubles the noble person. Taking no action that is not humane and engaging in no practice that is not courteous, the noble person, in case of a morning's troubles, would not be troubled."

] In an age of peace, Yu and Ji passed their own doors three times but did not enter.[14] Confucius praised them as worthies. In an age of disorder, Master Yan lived in a narrow lane, with a single bamboo basket of rice and a single gourd ladle of water. Others could not have endured his suffering, but Master Yan did not allow it to affect his joy. Confucius praised him as a worthy.[15]

Mencius said, "Yu, Ji, and Yan Hui were at one in the Way. Yu thought that if there were people drowning in the world, it was as if he were drowning them. Ji thought that if there were people starving in the world, it was as if he were starving them. This is why they were so anxious. Were Yu and Ji and Master Yan to have changed places, each would have acted in the same way.

"Now suppose some people who are lodging in the same house with me are quarreling: I go to save them. Though I do so with my cap tied on over unbound hair, this is acceptable. But if the people who are quarreling were merely from the same neighborhood, it would be questionable for me to go to save them with my cap tied on over unbound hair. Were I to close my door, that would be acceptable."

14. Commentators observe that "passing his door three times without entering" is an act of self-discipline usually ascribed to Yu, founder of the Xia. Here (Hou) Ji, one of the ancestors of the Zhou people, receives credit for the same action, apparently because he is often associated with Yu. See 3A4.
15. *Analects* 6:9.

[4B30] Master Gongdu said, "Throughout the state, everyone calls Kuang Zhang unfilial, yet you, Master, consort with him and treat him with courtesy. I dare to ask why this is."

Mencius said, "In the world today, there are five things that are considered unfilial. To be indolent in the use of one's four limbs and not concern oneself with the nurture of one's father and mother—this is the first form of unfiliality. To occupy oneself with chess and to be fond of drinking wine and not concern oneself with the nurture of one's father and mother—this is the second form of unfiliality. To be fond of goods and property and partial to one's wife and children and not concern oneself with the nurture of one's father and mother—this is the third form of unfiliality. To indulge the desires of the ears and eyes so as to disgrace one's father and mother—this is the fourth form of filiality. To be fond of bravery and to be quarrelsome and contentious, so as to endanger one's father and mother—this is the fifth form of unfiliality. Has Master Zhang done any one of these?

"Kuang Zhang and his father came to be at odds by demanding goodness of one another. To demand goodness of one another is the Way of friends. But for father and son to demand goodness of one another entails a great assault on affection. Kuang Zhang of course wanted to have good relations with his wife and children. But because he had offended his father and was not allowed to come near him, he sent away his wife and children and, for the rest of his life, has not had their nurture. He made up his mind that if it was not thus, this would be one of the greatest of crimes. This is Kuang Zhang."

[4B31] When Master Zeng was living in Wucheng, there were some marauders from Yue. Someone said, "Marauders are coming. Would it not be best to leave?"

Master Zeng said, "Do not lodge people in my house. They might damage the plants and trees."

When the marauders departed, he sent word: "Repair the walls of my house. I shall be returning." When the marauders had withdrawn, Master Zeng did return.

His attendants said, "Since the master was treated with such loyalty and respect, it was perhaps not right that, when the marauders came, he was the first to leave, in full view of the people, and that when the marauders departed, he returned." Shenyu Xing[16] said, "This is not something that you understand. I once had trouble with Fu Chu,[17] but none of the master's seventy disciples was involved in it."

When Zisi lived in Wei, there were marauders from Qi. Someone said, "Marauders are coming. Would it not be best to go?" Zisi said, "If I were to leave, who would there be to help the ruler protect the state?"

Mencius said, "Zengzi and Zisi were at one in the Way. Zengzi was a teacher—a father and an older brother. Zisi was a subject—the holder of a minor office. If Zengzi and Zisi were to have changed places, each would have acted in the same way."

2] Chuzi said, "The king sent someone to spy on the Master[18] to see whether he was different from other people." Mencius said, "How should I be different from other people? Yao and Shun were the same as other people."

3] A man of Qi had a wife and a concubine who lived together with him in his house. When the husband went out, he would always satiate his appetite for meat and drink before returning, and when his wife asked him with whom he ate and drank, it was always with prosperous and honorable people. The wife told the concubine, "When our good man goes out, he always satiates his appetite for meat and drink before returning, and when I ask him with whom he ate and drank, it is always with prosperous and honorable people. Yet no such people have ever appeared around here. I will observe our good man and see where he goes."

She arose early in the morning and followed her husband wherever he went. Nowhere in the city did anyone stand and talk with him. At last he came to the place in the eastern suburbs where people were

16. According to Zhao Qi, he was a disciple of Zengzi's.
17. According to Zhao Qi, Fu Chu was the name of a person. According to Zhu Xi, it referred to agricultural workers who carried grasses on their backs. D. C. Lau and Yang Bojun follow Zhao Qi, while James Legge follows Zhu Xi. Given the ambiguity, the text is difficult to interpret at this point.
18. That is, Mencius.

performing sacrifices at the graves. Here he begged for food, and when it was not enough, he looked around and went to another grave, this being his way of satiating his appetite.

His wife went back and told the concubine, "A husband is one to whom we look up and with whose life ours are forever bound. And now it turns out that he is like this. Together with the concubine she reviled the husband, and they wept together in the courtyard. The good man, knowing nothing of this, strutted in from outside, with an air of self-consequence, expecting to impress his wife and concubine.

From the point of view of the noble person, how few of those who seek wealth and honor, profit and success do so without giving good cause to their wives and concubines to weep together in shame!

BOOK 5A

1] Wan Zhang¹ asked, "When Shun went to the fields, weeping and crying out to merciful Heaven, why was it that he wept and cried?"

Mencius said, "It was from grief and longing."

Wan Zhang said, "When his father and mother love him, he should be glad and never forget them. If his father and mother hate him, 'though he may suffer, he should not be aggrieved.'² Was Shun then aggrieved?"³

Mencius said, "Chang Xi asked Gongming Gao,⁴ 'As to Shun's going to the fields, I have heard your instructions, but I do not know about his weeping and crying out to merciful Heaven and to his parents.' Gongming Gao said, 'This is something you do not understand.' Gongming Gao thought that the mind of the filial son could not be so dispassionate as this.⁵ [Shun said] 'In devoting my strength to tilling the fields, I am fulfilling my duties as a son, nothing more. What is there in me that causes my father and mother not to love me?'

1. A disciple of Mencius's.

2. The phrase *lao er bu yuan* 勞而不怨 (suffer but not be aggrieved) is found in the *Analects* 4:18.

3. The translation of the word *yuan* 怨 (here, "grief" or "aggrieved") is difficult. A more common translation for *yuan* is "resent" or "resentment," but this implies that the anger or dismay is directed outward—in this case at Shun's abusive parents. The significance of this passage turns, however, on Shun's remarkable ambivalence: he is apparently unsure whether the fault lies with them or with himself.

4. According to Zhu Xi, Chang Xi was a disciple of Kongming Gao's, who in turn was a disciple of Zengzi's.

5. Chang Xi's question to Gongming Gao is evidently construed by Mencius to imply that Chang, like Wan Zhang, thought that Shun should have shown no appearance of being aggrieved. The point here is that, while Shun was not *aggrieved*, it was only natural for him to be *grieved*.

"The sovereign, Yao, caused his children, nine sons and two daughters, his officers, oxen and sheep, granaries and storehouses, to be prepared to serve Shun in the channeled fields, and he was sought out by many of the men of service in the realm. It was the intention of the sovereign to have Shun join him in overseeing the realm and then to transfer it to him. But because he was not in harmony with his parents, Shun was like a poor man with no home to return to.

"To have the approval of the men of service of the realm is something everyone desires, yet this was not enough to dispel his sorrow. To have the love of women is something every man desires, and Shun had as wives the two daughters of the sovereign, yet this was not enough to dispel his sorrow. Wealth is something everyone desires, and he had the wealth that comes with possessing the realm, yet this was not enough to dispel his sorrow. Honor is something that everyone desires, and he had the honor of becoming the Son of Heaven, but this was not enough to dispel his sorrow. The reason why the approval of men, the love of women, wealth, and honor were not enough to dispel his sorrow was that it was a sorrow that could be dispelled only by being in harmony with his parents.

"A person when young longs for his father and mother; when he comes to know the love of women, he longs for young and beautiful women; when he has a wife and child, he longs for his wife and child. When he has an office, he longs for his ruler, and if he does not gain the regard of his ruler, he burns within. The person of great filial devotion longs throughout his life for his father and mother. In the great Shun there was manifested one who, at the age of fifty, still longed for them."

[5A2] Wan Zhang asked, "The ode says,

> To marry a wife, what should one do?
> He must inform his parents.[6]

"If it were truly as it says here, no one should have known it better than Shun. Why did Shun marry without informing them?"

---

6. Ode 101 (Legge, *Chinese Classics*, 4:155–57).

Mencius said, "If he had informed them, they would not have allowed him to marry. For a man and a woman to live together is the greatest of human relationships. To have informed his parents, and then to have had to forgo this greatest of human relationships, would have resulted in antagonism between him and his parents. This is why he did not inform them."

Wan Zhang said, "As to why Shun married without telling his parents, I have now received your instruction. But how was it that the sovereign, Yao, gave his daughters to Shun in marriage without having informed Shun's parents?"

"The sovereign, too, knew that if he informed them, he could not have given his daughters to Shun in marriage."

Wan Zhang said, "Shun's parents sent him to repair a granary, and, having removed the ladder, Shun's father, the Blind Man,[7] set the granary ablaze. They sent him to dig a well, and, having followed him out, they then covered it over. Shun's half brother, Xiang, said, 'Credit for the plan to immolate this lord-who-creates-capitals[8] rests solely with me. Let his oxen and sheep go to my parents, and also his storehouses and granaries. His spear will be mine; his lute will be mine; and his bow will be mine. My two sisters-in-law shall be put in charge of my women's quarters.' Xiang went to Shun's palace, and there was Shun on his couch, playing the lute. Xiang said, 'I have been concerned only for you, my lord.' He was embarrassed. Shun said, 'My sole concern has been for my subjects. You should govern them on my behalf.' Could it have been that Shun did not know that Xiang had tried to kill him?"

Mencius said, "How could he not have known? When Xiang was anxious, he, too, was anxious, and when Xiang was glad, he too was glad."

"Then was Shun just pretending to be glad?"

"No. Once, someone gave a live fish to Zichan of Zheng. Zichan instructed his pond keeper to put it into a fishpond, but the pond keeper cooked it. Going back to report, he said, 'When I first released it, it still seemed trapped, but after a little while it came into its own and joyfully

7. See 4A28, n. 28.
8. Zhu Xi's commentary explains that wherever Shun lived for three years became a capital, which accounts for Xiang's sarcastic description of him.

swam away.' Zichan said, 'It came into its element! It came into its element!' The pond keeper went out and said, 'Who says that Zichan is wise? I cooked the fish and ate it, and he said, "It came into its element! It came into its element!"'

"Thus, a noble man may be taken in by what is right, but he cannot be misled by what is contrary to the Way. Xiang came in the way that brotherly love should have impelled him to do, and therefore Shun believed him and was glad. In what way was he pretending?"

[5A3] Wan Zhang asked, "Xiang took as his daily occupation the cause of murdering Shun. Why, then, was it that Shun, upon becoming Son of Heaven, banished him?"[9]

Mencius said, "He enfeoffed him. Some referred to this as banishing him."

Wan Zhang said, "Shun sent the minister of works[10] to Youzhou and banished Huan Dou to Mount Chung. He put the Sanmiao[11] to death in Sanwei and imprisoned Kun[12] on Mount Yu. When he responded thus to the crimes of these four, everyone in the world was in agreement.[13] He had cut off those who were not humane. Yet Xiang, who was the most inhumane among them, was enfeoffed at Youbi. What crime had the people of Youbi committed? How could a humane person have done this? In the case of other people, he punished them, but when it came to his brother, he enfeoffed him."

9. Instead of punishing him for his misdeeds.

10. Referred to as Gong Gong, he appears in the "Canon of Yao," in the *Classic of Documents*, where he is recommended to Yao by Huan Dou. Yao's response is critical. See Legge, *Chinese Classics*, 3:23–24.

11. Presumably a people, with their ruler being the one punished by Shun. However, *Mencius* says that Shun killed (*sha* 殺) the Sanmiao, whereas the "Canon of Shun," in the *Classic of Documents*, says that he expelled (*cuan* 竄) them (Legge, *Chinese Classics*, 3:40).

12. The father of Yu, who would later become Shun's successor. Kun appears in the "Canon of Yao," *Classic of Documents*, as one who was assigned to deal with massive floods but who, after nine years, was unsuccessful (Legge, *Chinese Classics*, 3:24–25). In the "Canon of Shun," as in *Mencius*, the word used for Shun's punishment of Kun is *ji* 殛, which can mean either "to execute" or "to imprison for life" (ibid., 3:40). Zhu Xi favored the former interpretation.

13. With the exception of a single Chinese character, Wan Zhang's review of Shun's punishments follows the text of the "Canon of Shun" (Legge, *Chinese Classics*, 3:39–40).

"A humane man does not store up anger against his brother, nor harbor grievances against him. He simply loves him; that is all. Loving him, he desires him to be honored; loving him, he desires him to be wealthy. His enfeoffment at Youbi was to make Xiang wealthy and honored. If, while Shun himself was sovereign his brother had been a common man, could he be said to have loved him?"

"May I venture to ask what you meant when you said, 'Some referred to this as banishing him'?"

"Xiang could take no action in his state. The Son of Heaven appointed officials to administer the state and to collect the tribute and taxes from it, which is why it was called 'banishment.' How could he have been allowed to oppress the people? However, Shun frequently wanted to see him, and so there was a constant flow of people coming to court. This is what was meant by the saying, 'He did not wait for the time of tribute or for affairs of government to receive the lord of Youbi.'"

4] Xianqiu Meng[14] asked, "There is a saying that 'a ruler cannot regard a scholar of consummate Virtue as a subject, nor can a father regard him as a son.' Shun stood facing south, and Yao, at the head of all the lords, faced north and paid homage to him. Gusou also faced north and paid homage to him. When Shun saw Gusou, his countenance was disquieted. Confucius said, 'At this time all-under-Heaven was in danger—in imminent peril!' I do not know whether this is true."

Mencius said, "These are not the words of a noble person. They are the words of an uncultivated person from the east of Qi. When Yao was old, Shun assisted him. The 'Canon of Yao' says,

After twenty-eight years Fang Xun[15] died.
It was as if the people had lost a father or a mother.
For three years, no music[16] was heard within the four seas.[17]

14. According to Zhao Qi, he was a disciple of Mencius's.
15. That is, Yao.
16. Literally, the "eight sounds," referring to instruments made of metal, stone, cord, bamboo, calabash, earthenware, leather, or wood. See Legge, *Chinese Classics*, 2:352.
17. These sentences are found in what is now known as the "Canon of Shun" (ibid., 3:40–41).

Confucius said, 'In the sky there are not two suns, nor do the people have two kings.' If Shun had already become Son of Heaven before Yao died and also led the lords in all-under-Heaven in observing the three years' mourning for Yao, this would have meant there were two Sons of Heaven at the same time."

Xianqiu Meng said, "I have received your instruction about Shun's not treating Yao as a subject. Yet the ode says,

> There is no place under Heaven
> That is not the king's land.
> No one within the borders
> Who is not the king's subject.[18]

I venture to ask, When Shun became Son of Heaven, what could his father have been if not his subject?"

"This ode does not mean what you suggest. It speaks of laboring at the king's business and not being able to nurture one's parents. It says, 'This is all the king's business. Why am I alone worthy to serve?' Thus, in explaining an ode, one should not use a word to distort a phrase nor use a phrase to distort the overall intent. If one thinks about understanding the intent, one will get it. If one thinks solely in terms of phrases, there is the ode 'Milky Way,' which says,

> Of the black-haired people remaining from the Zhou
> Not a single one survived.[19]

If one took these words literally, the Zhou would have had no survivors.

"Of the attainments of a filial child, there is none greater than honoring one's parents, and among the honors paid to one's parents, there is none greater than nurturing them with all-under-Heaven. To be the father of the Son of Heaven is the ultimate honor, and to be nurtured with all-under-Heaven is the ultimate nurturing. This is what is meant by the ode when it says,

18. Ode 205 (ibid., 4:360–62).
19. Ode 258 (ibid., 4:528–34).

So long did he express his filial thoughts,
That his filial thoughts became a model.[20]

The *Classic of Documents* says,

Reverently performing his duties,
He appeared before Gusou—awestruck, fearful, grave.
And Gusou was also transformed.[21]

Can this be understood as a case of a father not treating a scholar of consummate Virtue as a son?"

5] Wan Zhang said, "Did it happen that Yao gave the realm to Shun?"

Mencius said, "No. The Son of Heaven cannot give the realm to someone."

"But Shun did possess the realm. Who gave it to him?"

"Heaven gave it to him."

"When Heaven gave it to him, did it ordain this through repeated instructions?"

"No. Heaven does not speak. This was manifested simply through Shun's actions and his conduct of affairs."

"In what way was this manifested through his actions and his conduct of affairs?"

"The Son of Heaven can present a man to Heaven, but he cannot cause Heaven to give him the realm. The lords can present a man to the Son of Heaven, but they cannot cause the Son of Heaven to make him a lord. A great officer can present a man to the lords, but he cannot cause the lords to make him a great officer. In antiquity Yao presented Shun to Heaven, and it was Heaven that accepted him. He displayed him to the people, and the people accepted him. This is why I said that 'Heaven does not speak.' This was manifested solely through his actions and his conduct of affairs."

---

20. Ode 243 (ibid., 4:458–60).

21. "Counsels of the Great Yu," *Classic of Documents* (ibid., 3:66). I follow Legge's sense of the term *yun* 允 but translate it as "transformed."

"I venture to ask how it was that Yao presented him to Heaven and Heaven accepted him, and he showed him to the people and the people accepted him?"

"He caused him to preside over the sacrifices, and the hundred spirits enjoyed them. This shows that Heaven accepted him. He put him in charge of affairs, and affairs were well ordered, and the hundred surnames[22] were at peace. This shows that the people accepted him. Heaven gave it to him; the people gave it to him. This is why I said that 'the Son of Heaven cannot give the realm to someone.' Shun assisted Yao for twenty-eight years. This is not something that could have been brought about by a human being. It was Heaven. After Yao died, and the three years' mourning was completed, Shun withdrew from Yao's son and went south of the South River. But the lords of the realm, when they went to court, went not to Yao's son but to Shun. Litigants went not to Yao's son but to Shun. Singers sang not of Yao's son but of Shun. This is why I said, 'It was Heaven.' It was after all this that he went to the central states and ascended to the position of the Son of Heaven. If he had just taken up residence in Yao's palace and ousted Yao's son, this would have been usurpation and not Heaven's gift. The 'Great Declaration' says,

The people are vectors of heavenly approval

> Heaven sees as my people see,
> Heaven hears as my people hear.[23]

"This is what was meant."

[5A6] Wan Zhang asked, "Some people say that Yu's Virtue was weak and he did not transmit the power to rule to someone worthy but rather to his own son. Is this true?"

Mencius said, "No, that is not true. When Heaven gave the power to rule to the worthiest, it was given to the worthiest. When Heaven gave it to a son, it was given to a son. Shun presented Yu to Heaven. Seventeen years passed, and Shun died. At the end of the three years'

---

22. The people as a whole.
23. See the "Taishi" chapter in the *Classic of Documents* (Legge, *Chinese Classics*, 3:292).

mourning, Yu withdrew from Shun's son to Yangcheng. The people of the realm followed Yu. It was as it was after Yao died and they did not follow Yao's son but followed Shun. Yu presented his minister, Yi, to Heaven, and after seven years, Yu died. At the end of the three years' mourning, Yi withdrew from Yu's son to the north of Mount Qi. Those going for an audience at court and those engaged in litigation did not follow Yi but followed Yu's son, Qi. They said, "This is the son of our ruler." The singers did not sing about Yi but sang about Qi, saying, "This is the son of our ruler."

"Danzhu[24] was not equal to his father, and Shun's son was also not equal to his father. Shun assisted Yao, and Yu assisted Shun, and as this went on over the course of years, they conveyed rich benefits upon the people over a long period of time. Qi was worthy and able reverently to continue the Way of Yu. Yi had assisted Yu for only a few years, and he had not been able to confer rich benefits upon the people for a long period of time. Shun and Yu differed from Yi in their periods of service, and their sons differed greatly in their worthiness. All this was owing to Heaven and was not something that could be brought about by human beings. What happens without anyone's causing it is owing to Heaven; what comes about without anyone's accomplishing it is the mandate.

"A common man who comes to possess all-under-Heaven must have Virtue comparable to that of Shun and Yu and also the recommendation of the Son of Heaven. This is why Confucius never possessed all-under-Heaven. One who has inherited all-under-Heaven is put aside only by Heaven if he is like Jie or *Zhou*. This is why Yi, Yi Yin, and the Duke of Zhou did not possess all-under-Heaven. Yi Yin assisted Tang in becoming king of all-under-Heaven. Tang died, and Tai Ding not having been appointed ruler, Wai Bing ruled for two years and Zhong Ren for four years. Tai Jia overturned the laws of Tang, and Yi Yin banished him to Tung for three years. Tai Jia came to regret his errors, to repent and redeem himself, dwelling in humaneness and reforming himself in rightness. After three more years, during which he listened to the instructions of Yi Yin, he returned to Bo.

24. Yao's son.

"That the Duke of Zhou did not possess all-under Heaven was like the case of Yi in the state of Xia or like Yi Yin in the Yin. Confucius said, 'In Tang and Yu,[25] the succession occurred through abdication; in Xia, Yin, and Zhou, it was hereditary. The principle is the same.'"

[5A7] Wan Zhang asked, "People say that Yi Yin sought the attention of Tang[26] through his cooking. Was this so?"

Mencius said, "No, it was not so. Yi Yin farmed in the lands of the ruler of Xin, and there he delighted in the Way of Yao and Shun. Had it involved anything contrary to rightness or to the Way, though he were offered rule over the empire, he would not have considered it, and though a thousand teams of horses were yoked for him, he would not have given them a glance. Had it involved anything contrary to rightness or to the Way, he would neither have given the smallest trifle to anyone nor accepted the smallest trifle from anyone. Tang sent a messenger with presents by way of entreaty, and, with utter indifference, Yi Yin said, 'What could I do with Tang's presents? Wouldn't it be better to be amidst these fields, delighting in the Way of Yao and Shun?'

"After Tang sent messengers three times to entreat him, he changed and, with altered countenance, said, 'Were I allowed to remain amidst these fields, I might delight in the Way of Yao and Shun. But might it not be better if I caused this ruler to become a Yao or a Shun? Might it not be better if I caused this people to become the people of Yao and Shun? Might it not be better if I saw these things for myself in my own person? Heaven, in giving birth to this people, causes those who are first to know to awaken those who are later to know and causes those who are first awakened to awaken those who are later to be awakened. I am one of those of Heaven's people who has awakened first; I will take this Way and use it to awaken this people. If I do not awaken them, who will do so?' He thought that if, among the people in the world, there was a common man or common woman who did not share in the benefits of Yao and Shun, it was as if he himself had pushed them into

25. Here Tang is the name of Yao's dynasty, and Yu is the name of Shun's dynasty.
26. First the tutor and later a minister to Tang the Accomplished, known as the first ruler of the Shang dynasty, Yi Yin is regarded as one of the exemplary ministers of Chinese history.

a ditch. So it was that he took upon himself the responsibility for the heavy weight of the world.[27]

"Therefore he went to Tang and spoke with him about attacking the Xia and saving the people.

"I have not heard of one who bent himself and, in so doing, straightened others. How much less could one disgrace himself and in so doing correct the world! The sages have differed in their actions. Some have kept their distance; others have approached. Some have departed; others have not. The point of convergence has been in keeping their persons pure, that is all. I have heard of seeking the attention of Tang through the Way of Yao and Shun; I have not heard of doing so through cooking.

"The 'Instructions of Yi' says,

Heaven began its punishment
With an attack on the Palace of Mu.
I began with Bo."[28]

[8]   Wan Zhang asked Mencius, "Some say that Confucius, while he was living in Wei, stayed with Yung Ju[29] and, while he was living in Qi, with the attendant[30] Ji Huan. Is this true?"

Mencius said, "No, it is not true. Such stories are devised by those who are fond of invention. When he was in Wei, he lived with Yen Chouyou. The wife of the officer Mi was the sister of the wife of Zilu, and officer Mi told Zilu, 'If Confucius stays with me, he should be able to become a high official of Wei.' Zilu told this to Confucius, who said, 'There is the Mandate.' Confucius advanced according to ritual and withdrew according to rightness. As to his attaining or not attaining

27. This passage is repeated in 5B1.
28. The text of the "Instructions of Yi" that appears in the *Classic of History* differs from what is quoted here. See Legge, *Chinese Classics*, 3:194. In any case, the point is that Heaven began its punishment in Jie's own palace due to his misdeeds, while Yi Yin began to translate Heaven's will into action in Bo by advising Tang, who would oust Jie and found the Shang dynasty.
29. A rather unlikely name. It means "ulcer."
30. According to Zhu Xi, the title refers to a eunuch.

office, he said, 'There is the Mandate.' If he had stayed with Yung Ju or the attendant Ji Huan, this would have been in accord neither with rightness nor with the Mandate.

"Not having been well received in Lu and in Wei, Confucius, on his departure, encountered Huan,[31] the master of horses in Song, who wanted to kill him. He passed through Song disguised in the clothing of a common man. At that time, though in circumstances of distress, he stayed with the city master Zhenzi, who was then an official of Zhou, the lord of Chen.

"I have heard that one may judge a person by those whom he hosts when he is at home and by those who host him when he is traveling. If Confucius had stayed with Yong Ju or the attendant Ji Huan, how would he have been Confucius?"

[5A9] Wan Zhang asked, "Some say that Boli Xi sold himself to an animal herder in Qin for the skins of five sheep and fed his oxen in order to procure an introduction to Duke Mu of Qin. Is this true?"

Mencius said, "It is not true. Such stories are devised by those who are fond of invention. Boli Xi was a man of Yu. The people of Jin offered Yu the jade ceremonial disk of Chui Ji and the horses of Qu as a means of borrowing a path through Yu in order to attack Guo. Gong Zhiqi remonstrated,[32] while Boli Xi did not. He knew that the Duke of Yu could not be remonstrated with, and so he left for Qin. This was when he was at the age of seventy. If he did not know that it would be contemptible to seek an introduction to Duke Mu of Qin through feeding oxen, could he be considered wise? As he did not remonstrate when he knew that remonstration would be of no use, could he be considered unwise? For knowing that the Duke of Yu was about to be destroyed and leaving him before that occurred, he cannot be considered unwise. Can he be considered to have been unwise when, having been elevated to high office in Qin and realizing that Duke Mu was someone with whom he could act, he then assisted him? As chief minister of Qin, he made his ruler prominent throughout the world

---

31. Or Huan Tui. See the *Analects* 7:22.
32. Against accepting the bribe from Jin.

and his own achievements worthy of being transmitted to later generations. Could he have done this if he were not a worthy man? As to
selling himself in order to promote his ruler, even a villager with any
self-esteem would not do this. And will you say that a worthy could
have done so?"

BOOK 5B

[5B1] Mencius said, "Boyi would not allow his eyes to look at a bad sight or his ears to listen to a bad sound. If he did not approve of a ruler, he would not serve him.[1] If he did not approve of a people, he would not lead them. When conditions were orderly, he would advance; when conditions were disorderly, he would retire. He could not bear to live in a court from which corrupt government emanated or in a place where corrupt people dwelled. He thought that being in the same place as a villager was like sitting in dirt and soot with his court robes and court cap on. In the time of Zhou, he lived by the shores of the northern sea, waiting for all-under-Heaven to be purified. Thus, when people hear about the character of Boyi, the compromised become pure and the weak acquire determination.

"Yi Yin said, 'What ruler may I not serve? What people may I not lead?' In times of good government, he came forward; in circumstances of disorder he also came forward. He said, 'Heaven, in giving birth to this people, causes those who are first to know to awaken those who are later to know and causes those who are first to be awakened to awaken those who are later to be awakened. I am one of Heaven's people who has awakened first; I will take this Way and use it to awaken this people.' He thought that if, among the people of the world, there was a common man or a common woman who did not share in the benefits bestowed by Yao and Shun, it was as if he himself had pushed them into a ditch. So it was that he took upon himself the responsibility for the heavy weight of the world.[2]

---

1. There is a similar characterization of Boyi in 2A9.
2. This passage is repeated from 5A7.

"Liuxia Hui was not ashamed of an impure ruler, nor did he disdain a minor office. When he was promoted, he did not conceal his abilities but resolutely carried out his Way. When he was passed over, he did not complain; when he was afflicted with poverty, he did not grieve. When he was with villagers, he was so entirely at ease that he could not bear to leave. He said, 'You are you, and I am I. Even if you were to stand by my side in a state of complete undress, how could you cause me to be defiled?[3] Thus, when people hear of the character of Liuxia Hui, the narrow-minded become liberal and the selfish become generous.

"When Confucius was leaving Qi, he strained the water off the rice that was to have been cooked and departed. When he left Lu, he said, 'In time, in time I shall depart.' This was the way to leave the state where his parents had lived. When it was right to act quickly, he was quick; when it was right to be deliberate, he was deliberate. When it was right to retire, he retired; when it was right to serve, he served. That was Confucius."

Mencius said, "Boyi was the sage who was pure; Yi Yin was the sage who was responsible; Liuxia Hui was the sage who was accommodating. Confucius was the sage who was timely. With Confucius there was the perfect ensemble.[4] The perfect ensemble begins with the sound of the bronze bell and ends with the sound of the jade chimes, the bronze bell anticipating the harmony at the beginning of the concert and the jade chimes bringing the harmony to a conclusion at its close. The harmony at the opening is the work of wisdom; the harmony at the close is the work of sageliness. Wisdom is like skill and sageliness is like strength. It is like shooting an arrow from a distance of a hundred paces. That you reach the target is a matter of strength; that you hit the mark is not a matter of strength."

B2] Bogong Qi asked, "How were the ranks of nobility and the emoluments arranged by the Zhou house?"

---

3. The language used to describe Liuxia Hui to this point is very close to the language used to describe him in 2A9.

4. "The perfect ensemble" is an attempt to capture the sense of the Chinese phrase *ji da cheng* 集大成. It is slightly more literal, though far less elegant, than James Legge's description of Confucius as a "complete concert."

Mencius said, "The details of it cannot be heard, as the feudal lords, disliking the records because they had been damaging to themselves, did away with them. Yet the essentials of it I have heard. The Son of Heaven represented one rank; the dukes one rank; the marquises, one rank; the earls, one rank; the viscounts and the barons shared one rank. Altogether there were five levels. The ruler represented one rank; the chief ministers, one rank; the great officers, one rank; the scholars of the highest grade, one rank; the scholars of the middle grade, one rank; the scholars of the lower grade, one rank. Altogether there were six levels. The land allotted to the Son of Heaven was a thousand *li* square; the land allotted to the dukes and marquises was in all cases a hundred *li*; to the earls and viscounts, seventy *li*; to the barons, fifty *li*. Altogether there were four levels. One who could not have fifty *li* could not have access to the Son of Heaven but, being attached to one of the marquises, was called a 'dependent.'

"The chief ministers of the Son of Heaven received land equivalent to that of the marquises; the great officers received land equivalent to that of the earls; a scholar of the first rank received land equivalent to that of a viscount or a baron. In a great state, in which the territory was a hundred *li* square, the ruler had an emolument ten times that of the chief minister; the chief minister, an emolument four times that of the great officers; a great officer, twice that of a scholar of the highest grade; a scholar of the highest grade, twice that of a scholar of the middle grade; a scholar of the middle grade, twice that of a scholar of the lower grade; a scholar of the lower grade, the same emolument as an ordinary person serving in an official position, an emolument sufficient to compensate for what would have been earned tilling the fields.

"In a state of the next size, with a territory equal to seventy *li*, the ruler would have ten times the emolument of the chief minister; a chief minister three times that of a great officer; a great officer, twice that of a scholar of the highest grade; a scholar of the highest grade, twice that of a scholar of the middle grade; a scholar of the middle grade, twice that of a scholar of the lower grade; a scholar of the lower grade, the same emolument as an ordinary person serving in an official position, an emolument sufficient to compensate for what would have been earned tilling the fields.

"In a small state, with a territory equal to fifty *li*, the ruler would have an emolument ten times that of the chief minister; a chief minister, twice that of a great officer; a great officer, twice that of a scholar of the highest rank; a scholar of the highest rank, twice that of a scholar of the middle rank; a scholar of the middle rank, twice that of a scholar of the lower rank; a scholar of the lower grade, the same emolument as an ordinary person serving in an official position, an emolument sufficient to compensate for what he would have been earned tilling the fields.

"As to the tillers of the fields, each received a hundred *mu*. With an allotment of a hundred *mu*, the most capable tillers could feed nine people; the next level, eight; the next level, seven; the next level, six; and the lowest level, five. The emoluments of ordinary people serving in office were adjusted according to this."

3] Wan Zhang asked, "May I ask about friendship?"

Mencius said, "In friendship one should not presume upon one's own seniority, high rank, or the prestige of one's family connections. To befriend someone is to befriend his Virtue, which allows for no such presumption.

"Meng Xianzi was from a family of a hundred chariots. He had five friends, including Yuezheng Qiu, Mu Zhong, and three others whose names I have forgotten. Xianzi had a friendship with these five because they did not think about Xianzi's family. If these five had thought about Xianzi's family, they would not have been his friends. This happens not only in the case of a family with a hundred chariots. It may happen in the case of the ruler of a small state, as when Duke Hui of Bi said, 'I treat Zisi as my teacher; I treat Yan Ban as my friend; Wang Xun and Chang Xi are men who serve me.' It is not only in the case of a ruler of a small state that this happens. It may happen in the case of the ruler of a large state, as with Duke Ping of Jin and Hai Tang. When Hai Tang told the duke to enter, he entered. When he told him to sit, he sat. When he told him to eat, he ate. Even if it was just coarse rice and a vegetable soup, he always ate his fill because he did not dare not to do so. But this is as far as he went. He never asked him to share in Heaven's ranks, to govern Heaven's offices, or to receive Heaven's emoluments. This was honoring the worthy in the manner of a man of service, not honoring the worthy in the manner of a king or a duke.

"Shun went up to see the emperor, and the emperor lodged him as his son-in-law in the second palace. The emperor offered him hospitality, and they alternated with one another as guest and host. This was a friendship between the Son of Heaven and an ordinary man.

"The respect given by subordinates to superiors is called honoring the honorable. The respect given by superiors to subordinates is called esteeming the worthy. In both cases the principle is the same."

[5B4] Wan Zhang said, "May I ask what is the attitude of mind expressed in social interchange?"

Mencius said, "Respect."

"Why is it that declining a gift is considered disrespectful?"

"When it is given by an estimable person yet one receives it only after asking oneself, 'Did he get it by righteous or unrighteous means?' this is considered disrespectful. Therefore one does not decline."

"If one does not say so overtly but declines a gift in one's mind, saying to oneself that 'this was taken from the people unrighteously,' may one not refuse to accept it while adducing some other reason for refusing?"

"If the association was according to the Way, and the gift was offered according to ritual, Confucius would have accepted it."

"Now, here is someone who waylays people outside the gates of the city. If his association with you is according to the Way, and his gift is offered according to ritual, is it right to accept it?"

"It is *not* right. It says in the 'Announcement to Kang,'

Those who kill people and rob them,
Fierce men for whom death holds no fear,
Are universally hated among the people.[5]

Such as these are to be punished without any prior attempt to reform them. This practice has been handed down from the Xia to the Yin and from the Yin to the Zhou, without change. Yet the crime of rob-

---

5. The quotation from the "Announcement to Kang," in the *Classic of Documents*, is inexact. See Legge, *Chinese Classics*, 3:392.

bery persists right down to today. How could one accept the gift of a robber?"[6]

"The lords of today, as they take from the people, are much like the highwaymen, but if they are familiar with ritual, the lords will accept them. May I ask how you explain this?"

"Do you think that if a true king should arise, he would have all the lords of today put to death? Or would he teach them and then put to death those who remained unreformed? To call anyone who takes what is not his a robber is to expand the category of robbery and to extend rightness to its outermost limits."

"When Confucius was in Lu, the people of Lu fought over the game taken in hunting, and Confucius also fought over it. If that fight for captured game was permissible, how much more so receiving gifts offered by the lords?"

"Then, when Confucius served in office, it was not with the idea of carrying his teachings into practice?"

"It was with the idea of carrying his teachings into practice."

"If it *was* with the idea of carrying his teachings into practice, how did he become involved in fighting over captured game?"

"Confucius first laid down rules for sacrificial vessels based on the records and did not allow them to be filled with food gathered from the four quarters."

"Why did he not go away?"

"He was attempting a trial. When the trial showed that it could work, yet it did not work, he left. This is why he never spent three years in any one state. Confucius took office when he saw that the practice of his teachings was possible, when he was treated with due ceremony, or when he was supported by the state. With Ji Huan, he took office on seeing that his teachings might be implemented. With Duke Ling of Wei, he was treated ceremoniously, and with Duke Xiao of Wei, he was supported by the state."

B5] Mencius said, "The point of serving in office is not to avoid poverty, but there are times when one does serve owing to poverty. The point of

6. The text appears to be corrupt at this point, and the preceding three sentences of translation are very tentative.

entering into marriage is not to be cared for, but there are times when one does marry owing to the need to be cared for. One who is poor will decline an honorable position and accept a humble one; he will reject wealth and remain in poverty. What office would be suitable for one who is to decline an honorable position and accept a humble one, to reject wealth and remain in poverty—that of a gatekeeper or a watchman? Confucius once served as a storekeeper. What he said was, 'My calculations must be correct; that is all.' He was once in charge of public fields. What he said was, 'The oxen and sheep must grow, increase, and be strong; that is all.' To occupy a humble position and speak of lofty matters is a crime. To stand in the ruler's court and not have the Way carried into practice is shameful."

[5B6] Wan Zhang asked, "Why does a man of service not become a protégé of one of the lords?"

Mencius said, "He does not presume to do so. If a lord loses his state and then puts himself under the protection of another lord, this is according to ritual. But for a man of service to become the protégé of a lord is not according to ritual."

Wan Zhang said, "If a ruler sends him a gift of grain, does he accept it?"

"He accepts it."

"According to what understanding of rightness does he accept it?"

"A lord provides charity for one who comes from another state."

"Why does he accept charity while he does not accept payment?"

"He does not presume to do so."

"I presume to ask why he does not presume to do so?"

"Gatekeepers or watchmen all have regular employment for which they accept support from on high. Not to have regular employment and yet to receive payment from on high would be considered disrespectful."

"Suppose a ruler sends a gift, and it is accepted. I wonder how long such a practice can be continued?"

"Take the case of Duke Mu and Zisi. The duke often inquired about Zisi and often sent gifts of meat for the tripod. Zisi was not pleased, and in the end turned the messenger out of the great door and, facing north and twice knocking his head on the ground, he refused the gift, saying, 'Now, I know that the duke treats me like his horses and dogs.' It seems that it was from this time[7] that the gifts stopped coming. "If a ruler is pleased with a person of worth and ability but can neither promote nor support him, can he be said to be pleased with the worthy?"

"I presume to ask how the ruler of a state should act if he wishes to support a noble person in a way that can truly be regarded as support?"

"At first the gift is presented at the ruler's command. The man of service, knocking his head twice on the ground, receives it. Thereafter, the storekeeper continues to send grain, and the keeper of the kitchen continues to send meat, but not as if it were coming at the ruler's command. Zisi thought that receiving meat from the ruler's tripod, which caused him to have the constant annoyance of doing obeisance, was not the way to support a noble person.

"In the case of Yao and Shun, Yao caused his nine sons to serve Shun and his two daughters to marry him. He caused the hundred officers, oxen and sheep, storehouses and granaries to be prepared to support Shun as he worked in the channeled fields. Thereafter, he raised him to the highest position. This is why we speak of 'honoring the worthy in the manner of a king or a duke.' "[8]

B7] Wan Zhang said, "I presume to ask what rightness is involved in not going to see one of the lords?"[9]

Mencius said, "One who lives in the city is called a 'subject of the marketplace and wells,' while one living in the wilds is called a 'subject of grass and plants.' In both cases they are called 'commoners,' and a commoner who has not yet submitted his introductory present and become a minister does not presume to have an interview with the lord. This is according to ritual."

Wan Zhang said, "How is it that a common man, when summoned to perform some service, goes and performs it, while a scholar, when summoned by a ruler who wishes to see him, will not go?"

7. Reading beginning (*shi* 始) for lookout tower or title of respect (*tai* 臺).
8. See 5B3.
9. Gongsun Chou asks the same question of Mencius in 3B7.

"To go and perform the service would be right. To go to see the ruler would not be right. And why is it that the ruler wishes to see him?"

"Both because he is well informed and because he is worthy."

"If it is because he is well informed, even the Son of Heaven would not summon a teacher, much less would one of the lords. And if it is because of his worthiness, I have not heard of anyone wishing to see a worthy man and summoning him.

"Duke Mu often saw Zisi. Once he said, 'In antiquity, the ruler of a state of a thousand chariots would have been friendly with scholars. What do you think of that?' Zisi was not pleased and said, 'The ancients said, "A scholar should be served." How could they have said, "Make him your friend"?' Being thus displeased, how could Zisi *not* have said, 'In terms of our positions, you are the ruler, and I am the subject. How could I presume to be a friend of the ruler? In terms of our Virtue, you should be serving me. How could you be my friend?' Thus a ruler with a thousand chariots may have sought to be a friend of a scholar, but he could not do so, much less summon him to his presence.

"Once, when Duke Jing of Qi was hunting, he summoned the game-keeper with a flag. The gamekeeper would not come, and the duke was about to have him killed. 'The dedicated officer does not forget that he may end up in a ditch; the courageous officer does not forget that he may sacrifice his head.' What was the point that Confucius drew from this? It was the gamekeeper's refusal to go in response to an inappropriate summons.[10]

"I presume to ask what should be used to summon a gamekeeper?"

"He is to be summoned with a leather cap, a commoner with a flag, a man of service with a banner, and a great officer with a pennon. When the gamekeeper was summoned with the pennon appropriate for summoning a great officer, he would sooner have died than have presumed to go. If a commoner were summoned with the banner appropriate for summoning a man of service, how would the commoner have presumed to go—how much less a worthy man who is summoned by a means not befitting such a man?

10. This example, in almost identical language, is invoked also in 3B1.

"If a ruler wishes to see a worthy man but does not go about it in accordance with the Way, it is like wanting him to enter and yet closing the door. Now, rightness is the road and ritual is the door. Only a noble person can follow this road and enter and depart by this door. The ode says,

> The way to Zhou is like a whetstone,
> And straight as an arrow.
> The noble person treads it,
> The small person looks on it.[11]

Wan Zhang said, "When Confucius was summoned by the ruler's command, he went without waiting for the horses to be harnessed. Was Confucius wrong to have done so?"

"Confucius was at that time holding office and had official duties. And it was in his official capacity that he was summoned."

8] Mencius said to Wan Zhang, "That scholar, whose goodness is most outstanding in the village, will become a friend to all the good scholars of the village. That scholar, whose goodness is most outstanding in the state, will become a friend to all the good scholars of the state. That scholar, whose goodness is the most outstanding in the world, will become a friend to all the good scholars of the world. When he feels that being a friend of all the good scholars of the world is not enough, he will go back in time to consider the people of antiquity, repeating their poems and reading their books. Not knowing what they were like as persons, he considers what they were like in their own time. This is to go back in time and make friends."

9] King Xuan of Qi asked about high ministers.
Mencius said, "Which high ministers is the king asking about?"
The king said, "Are the ministers not the same?"

---

11. Ode 203. Translation adapted from Legge, *Chinese Classics*, 4:353. The ode itself seems clearly to have a retrospective quality to it—a lament for better days now long gone. As quoted in *Mencius*, the ode seems to have contemporary significance.

"They are not the same. There are ministers who are from the royal line and ministers who are of other surnames."

The king said, "May I inquire about those who are of the royal line?"

"If the ruler has great faults, they should remonstrate with him. If, after they have done so repeatedly, he does not listen, they should depose him."

The king suddenly changed countenance.

"You should not misunderstand. You inquired of me, your minister, and I dare not respond except truthfully."

The king's countenance became composed once again, and he then inquired about high ministers of a different surname.

"If the ruler has faults, they should remonstrate with him. If they do so repeatedly, and he does not listen, they should leave."

BOOK 6A

1] Gaozi said, "Human nature is like the willow tree; rightness is like cups and bowls. To make humaneness and rightness out of human nature is like making cups and bowls out of the willow tree."

humaneness as internal vs. external

Mencius said, "Are you able to make cups and bowls while following the nature of the willow tree? You must do violence to the willow tree before you can make cups and bowls. If you must do violence to the willow tree in order to make cups and bowls, must you also do violence to human beings in order to bring forth humaneness and rightness? The effect of your words will be to cause everyone in the world to think of humaneness and rightness as misfortunes."

2] Gaozi said, "Human nature is like swirling water. Open a passage for it in the east, and it will flow east; open a passage for it in the west, and it will flow west. Human nature does not distinguish between good and not-good any more than water distinguishes between east and west."

Mencius said, "It is true that water does not distinguish between east and west, but does it fail to distinguish between up and down? The goodness of human nature is like the downward course of water. There is no human being lacking in the tendency to do good, just as there is no water lacking in the tendency to flow downward. Now, by striking water and splashing it, you may cause it to go over your head, and by damming and channeling it, you can force it to flow uphill. But is this the nature of water? It is force that makes this happen. While people can be made to do what is not good, what happens to their nature is like this."

3] Gaozi said, "Life is what is called nature."

Mencius said, "When you say that 'life is what is called nature,' is this like saying that 'white is what is called white'?"

"Yes."

"Is the whiteness of a white feather like the whiteness of snow, and the whiteness of snow like the whiteness of white jade?"

"Yes."

"Then is the nature of a dog like the nature of an ox, and the nature of an ox like the nature of a human being?"

[6A4] Gaozi said, "The appetites for food and sex are human nature. Humaneness is internal rather than external; rightness is external rather than internal."

Mencius said, "Why do you say that humaneness is internal while rightness is external?"

Gaozi said, "One who is older than I, I treat as an elder. This is not because there is in me some sense of respect due to elders. It is like something being white and my recognizing it as white; I am responding to the whiteness, which is external. Therefore I call rightness external."

Mencius said, "There is no difference between the whiteness of a white horse and the whiteness of a white man. But is there no difference between the age of an old horse and the age of an old man? What is it that we speak of as rightness—the man's being old or my regarding him with the respect due to one who is old?"

Gaozi said, "Here is my younger brother; I love him. There is the younger brother of a man from Qin; him I do not love. The feeling derives from me, and therefore I describe it as internal. I treat an elder from Chu as old, just as I treat our own elders as old. The feeling derives from their age, and therefore I call it external."

Mencius said, "Our fondness for the roast meat provided by a man of Qin is no different from our fondness for the roast meat provided by one of our own people. Since this is also the case with a material thing, will you say that our fondness for roast meat is external as well?"

[6A5] Meng Jizi asked Gongduzi, "Why do you say that rightness is internal?"

Gongduzi said, "We are enacting our respect, and therefore it is internal."

"Suppose there were a villager who was one year older than your older brother—whom would you respect?"

"I would respect my older brother."

"For whom would you pour wine first when serving at a feast?"

"I would pour it first for the villager."

"You respect the one, but treat the other as older. So in the end, rightness is external and not internal."

Gongduzi, being unable to reply, told Mencius about it. Mencius said, "Ask him, whom does he respect more, his uncle or his younger brother? He will say that he respects his uncle. You then ask him, if his younger brother were impersonating the deceased at a sacrifice, whom would he respect more? He will say that he would respect his younger brother. Then ask, where is the respect due to his uncle? He will say that it is because of his younger brother's position that he shows him greater respect. Then you may also say that it is because of the position of the villager that you show him respect. While ordinarily the respect belongs to your brother, on occasion the respect belongs to the villager."

Jizi heard this and said, "When respect is due to my uncle, I show him respect; when respect is due to my brother, I show the respect to him. So respect is after all determined by externals and is not internally motivated."

Gongduzi said, "In the winter we drink hot water, while in the summer we drink cold water. Does this mean that drinking and eating too are externally determined?"

A6] Gongduzi said, "Gaozi said that human nature is neither good nor not-good. Others say that human nature can be made to be good or not-good, which is why, during the reigns of Kings Wen and Wu, the people were inclined to goodness, whereas under the reigns of You and Li, the people were inclined to violence. Still others say that the natures of some are good and the natures of others are not good, which is why, when Yao was the ruler, there could be Xiang,[1] while, with a father like

---

1. According to this view of human nature, which is obviously not that of Mencius, the fact that a violent man like Xiang could have lived during the reign of the sage-king Yao is evidence that people differ widely in their natures. Xiang was the depraved brother of Yao's exemplary successor, Shun.

Gusou, there could be Shun,[2] and with *Zhou*[3] as the son of their older brother as well as their ruler, there could be Qi, the Viscount of Wei, and Prince Bigan. Now, you say that human nature is good. Does this mean that these others are all wrong?"

Mencius said, "One's natural tendencies enable one to do good; this is what I mean by human nature being good. When one does what is not good, it is not the fault of one's native capacities. The mind of pity and commiseration is possessed by all human beings; the mind of shame and dislike is possessed by all human beings; the mind of respectfulness and reverence is possessed by all human beings; and the mind that knows right and wrong is possessed by all human beings. The mind of pity and commiseration is humaneness; the mind of shame and dislike is rightness; the mind of respectfulness and reverence is propriety; and the mind that knows right and wrong is wisdom. Humaneness, rightness, propriety, and wisdom are not infused into us from without. We definitely possess them. It is just that we do not think about it, that is all. Therefore it is said, "Seek and you will get it; let go and you will lose it."[4] That some differ from others by as much as twice, or five times, or an incalculable order of magnitude is because there are those who are unable fully to develop their capacities. The ode says,

> Heaven, in giving birth to humankind,
> Created for each thing its own rule.
> The people's common disposition
> Is to love this admirable Virtue.[5]

Confucius said, 'How well the one who made this ode knew the Way!' Therefore, for each thing, there must be a rule, and people's common disposition is therefore to love this admirable Virtue."

---

2. Gusou, the Blind Man, was the paradigm of the cruel father, to whom Shun nonetheless remained filial and devoted.

3. *Zhou*, the last ruler of the Shang dynasty, was universally believed to have been a monstrous tyrant. His older brother, Qi, and his uncle, Bigan, attempted, with notable lack of success, to counsel him.

4. See also the statement attributed to Confucius at the end of 6A8.

5. Ode 260 (Legge, *Chinese Classics*, 4:541–45).

7] Mencius said, "In years of abundance, most of the young people have the wherewithal to be good, while in years of adversity, most of them become violent. This is not a matter of a difference in the native capacities sent down by Heaven but rather of what overwhelms their minds.

"Now, let barley be sown and covered with earth; the ground being the same, and the time of planting also the same, it grows rapidly, and in due course of time,[6] it all ripens. Though there may be differences in the yield, this is because the fertility of the soil, the nourishment of the rain and the dew, and the human effort invested are not the same.

"Things of the same kind are thus like one another. Why is it that we should doubt this only when it comes to human beings? The sage and we are the same in kind. So Longzi[7] said, 'If someone makes shoes without knowing the size of a person's feet, I know that he will not make baskets.' That shoes are similar is because everyone in the world has feet that are alike. And when it comes to taste, all mouths are alike in their preferences. Yi Ya was first to apprehend what all mouths prefer. If, with regard to the way mouths are disposed to tastes, human nature differed from person to person, as is the case with dogs and horses differing from us in kind, why should it be that everyone in the world follows Yi Ya in matters of taste? The fact that everyone in the world takes Yi Ya as the standard in matters of taste is because we all have mouths that are similar. It is likewise with our ears: when it comes to sounds, everyone in the world takes Music Master Kuang as the standard because the ears of everyone in the world are similar. And so likewise with our eyes: when it comes to Zidu,[8] there is no one in the world who fails to recognize his beauty because one who failed to recognize the beauty of Zidu would have to be without eyes. Therefore I say mouths find savor in the same flavors; ears find satisfaction in the same sounds; eyes find pleasure in the same beauty. When it comes to

6. David S. Nivison takes *zhi yu ri zhi zhi shi* 至於日至之時 to mean "by midsummer," with *ri zhi* meaning "the summer solstice" ("On Translating Mencius," in *The Ways of Confucianism: Investigations in Chinese Philosophy*, ed. Bryan W. Van Norden [La Salle, Ill.: Open Court, 1996], 184).

7. See 3A3.

8. A man famous for his good looks.

our minds, could they alone have nothing in common? And what is it that our minds have in common? It is order and rightness.[9] The sage is just the first to apprehend what our minds have in common. Thus order and rightness please our minds in the same way that meat pleases our mouths."

[6A8] Mencius said, "The trees on Ox Mountain were once beautiful. But being situated on the outskirts of a large state, the trees were cut down by axes. Could they remain beautiful? Given the air of the day and the night, and the moisture of the rain and the dew, they did not fail to put forth new buds and shoots, but then cattle and sheep came along to graze upon them. This accounts for the barren appearance of the mountain. Seeing this barrenness, people suppose that the mountain was never wooded. But how could this be the nature of the mountain? So it is also with what is preserved in a human being: could it be that anyone should lack the mind of humaneness and rightness? If one lets go of the innate good mind, this is like taking an ax to a tree; being cut down day after day, can [one's mind] remain beautiful? Given the rest that one gets in the day and the night, and the effect of the calm morning *qi*, one's likes and dislikes will still resemble those of other people, but barely so. And then one can become fettered and destroyed by what one does during the day; if this fettering occurs repeatedly, the effect of the night *qi* will no longer be enough to allow one to preserve his mind, and he will be at scant remove from the animals. Seeing this, one might suppose that he never had the capacity for goodness. But can this be a human being's natural tendency? Thus, given nourishment, there is nothing that will not grow; lacking nourishment, there is nothing that will not be destroyed. Confucius said, 'Hold on and you preserve it; let

9. Following A. C. Graham, Nivison points to a parallel here with a passage in chap. 4 of the *Lushi chunqiu* (*The Springs and Autumns of Master Lu*), in which the hedonist Zihuazi is quoted as saying: " 'True kings enjoy the conduct by which they rise to power, the ruined likewise enjoy the conduct by which they are ruined.' . . . If this is so, true kings have a taste for order and duty, the ruined likewise have a taste for tyranny and idleness. Their tastes are not the same, so their fortunes are not the same" (A. C. Graham, "The Background of the Mencian (Mengzian) Theory of Human Nature," cited in Nivison, "On Translating Mencius," 183–84).

it go and you lose it. The time of its going out and coming in is not fixed, and there is no one who knows the place where it goes.' In saying this, he was referring to the mind."

9] Mencius said, "The king's lack of wisdom is hardly surprising. Take something that is the easiest thing in the world to grow. Expose it to the heat for a day, and then expose it to cold for ten days. It will not be able to grow. I see the king but seldom, and when I withdraw, the agents of cold arrive. Even if I have caused some buds to appear, what good does it do?

"Now, chess is one of the minor arts, but without concentrating one's mind and applying one's will, one cannot succeed in it. Chess Qiu is the finest chess player anywhere in the state; suppose that Chess Qiu is teaching two people to play chess. One of them concentrates his mind and applies his will, listening only to Chess Qiu. The other, while listening to him, is actually occupying his whole mind with a swan that he believes is approaching. He thinks about bending his bow, fitting his arrow, and shooting the swan. While he is learning alongside the other man, he does not compare with him. Is this because his intelligence is not comparable? I would say that this is *not* so."

10] Mencius said, "I desire fish, and I also desire bear's paws. If I cannot have both of them, I will give up fish and take bear's paws. I desire life, and I also desire rightness. If I cannot have both of them, I will give up life and take rightness. It is true that I desire life, but there is something I desire more than life, and therefore I will not do something dishonorable in order to hold on to it. I detest death, but there is something I detest more than death, and therefore there are some dangers I may not avoid. If, among a person's desires, there were none greater than life, then why should he not do anything necessary in order to cling to life? If, among the things he detested, there were none greater than death, why should he not do whatever he had to in order to avoid danger? There is a means by which one may preserve life, and yet one does not employ it; there is a means by which one may avoid danger, and yet one does not adopt it.

"Thus there are things that we desire more than life and things that we detest more than death. It is not exemplary persons alone who have this mind; all human beings have it. It is only that the exemplary ones are able to avoid losing it; that is all.

"Suppose there are a basketful of rice and a bowlful of soup. If I get them, I may remain alive; if I do not get them, I may well die. If they are offered contemptuously, a wayfarer will decline to accept them; if they are offered after having been trampled upon, a beggar will not demean himself by taking them.[10] And yet when it comes to a stipend of ten thousand *zhong*, I accept them without regard for decorum and rightness. What do the ten thousand *zhong* add to me? Is it because I can then get beautiful dwellings that I take them, or the service of wives and concubines, or the gratitude of poor acquaintances that I share them with? What formerly I would not accept even at the risk of death, I now accept for the sake of beautiful houses. What formerly I would not accept even at the risk of death, I now accept for the service of wives and concubines. What formerly I would not accept even at the risk of death, I now accept for the gratitude of poor acquaintances. Could such things not have been declined as well? This is what is called 'losing one's original mind.'"

[6A11] Mencius said, "Humaneness is the human mind. Rightness is the human path. To quit the path and not follow it, to abandon this mind and not know enough to seek it, is indeed lamentable. If a man has chickens and dogs that become lost, he knows enough to seek them. But when he has lost his mind, he does not know enough to seek it. The way of learning is none other than this: to seek for the lost mind."

[6A12] Mencius said, "Now suppose there is a person whose fourth finger is bent so that it cannot be straightened. This may be neither painful nor incapacitating, and yet, if there is someone who is able to straighten it,

---

10. Most interpret Mencius to be saying that wayfarers or beggars simply would rather die than take food they must have in order to live if it is not given in a polite manner. The passage can be read, as it is here, as saying that wayfarers or beggars *could* die without food they desperately need, and they are willing to *risk* death if it is offered in a demeaning manner. There is a story in the *Liji* (*Book of Rites*) that suggests this more plausible reading. The *Liji* story is set in a time of famine. Someone is handing out food on the road but in an unintentionally demeaning manner. One man rejects the food that is rudely given, refuses to accept it even after an apology, and ends up dying. See the "Tangong" chapter in James Legge, trans., *Li Chi: Book of Rites* (repr., New York: University Books, 1967), 1:194–95.

the afflicted person will not consider the road from Qin to Chu too far to go because his finger is not like other people's. When one's finger is unlike the fingers of others, one knows enough to hate it, but when one's mind is not like the minds of others, one does not know enough to hate it. This is what is called a failure to understand distinctions."

13] Mencius said, "Anyone who wants to grow a tung tree, or a catalpa, which can be grasped with the hands, will know how to nourish it. But when it comes to one's person, one does not know how to nourish it. Could it be that one's love for one's own person is not comparable to one's love for the tung or the catalpa? What a failure to think!"

14] Mencius said, "Human beings love all parts of themselves equally, and loving all parts equally, nurture all parts equally. There being not an inch of flesh that one does not love, there is not an inch of flesh one does not nurture. In examining whether one is good at it or not, the only way is to observe what one chooses in oneself.

"Some parts of the body are superior and others inferior; some are small and others are great. One should not harm the great for the sake of the small, nor should one harm the superior for the sake of the inferior. One who nurtures the smaller part of oneself becomes a small person, while one who nurtures the greater part of oneself becomes a great person.

"Here is a master gardener who neglects his *wu* 梧 and *jia* 檟 trees while nurturing thorns and brambles: he is an inferior gardener. Here is a person who, unknowingly, nurtures a single finger while neglecting his back and shoulders: he is a confused animal. A person given to drinking and eating is considered by others to be inferior because he nourishes what is small in himself while neglecting what is great. Would a person who, while drinking and eating, was not neglectful, regard his mouth and stomach as just an inch of flesh?"

15] Gongduzi asked, "All are equally persons, and yet some are great persons and others are small persons—why is this?"

Mencius said, "Those who follow the part of themselves that is great become great persons, while those who follow the part that is small become small persons."

Gongduzi said, "Since all are equally persons, why is it that some follow the part of themselves that is great while others follow the part that is small?"

Mencius said, "The faculties of hearing and sight do not think and are obscured by things. When one thing comes into contact with another, it is led astray. The faculty of the mind is to think. By thinking, it apprehends; by not thinking, it fails to apprehend. This is what Heaven has given to us. If we first establish the greater part of ourselves, then the smaller part is unable to steal it away. It is simply this that makes the great person."

[6A16] Mencius said, "There is the nobility of Heaven and the nobility of man. Humaneness, rightness, loyalty, and truthfulness—and taking pleasure in doing good, without ever wearying of it— this is the nobility of Heaven. The ranks of duke, minister, or high official—this is the nobility of man. Men of antiquity cultivated the nobility of Heaven and the nobility of man followed after it. Men of the present day cultivate Heavenly nobility out of a desire for the nobility of man, and, once having obtained the nobility of man, they cast away the nobility of Heaven. Their delusion is extreme, and, in the end, they must lose everything."

[6A17] Mencius said, "In their desire to be honored, human beings are of like mind. And all human beings have in themselves what is honorable. It is only that they do not think about it; that is all. The honor that derives from men is not the original, good honor. Whom Zhao Meng honors, Zhao Meng can also debase. The ode says,

> We have been plied with wine,
> And satisfied with Virtue.[11]

To satisfy with virtue means that one is satisfied with humaneness and rightness, and therefore does not crave the flavors of the meat and grain served by men, and when a good reputation and widespread esteem accrue to one's person, one does not crave the elegant embroidered garments worn by men."

11. Ode 247 (Legge, *Chinese Classics*, 4:475–78).

8] Mencius said, "Humaneness overcomes inhumaneness just as water overcomes fire. Those today who practice humaneness do it as if they were using a cup of water to put out the fire consuming a cartload of firewood, and then, when the flames are not extinguished, they say that water does not overcome fire. This is to make an enormous concession to what is not humane, and in the end it must inevitably result in the destruction of humaneness."

9] Mencius said, "The five kinds of grain are the finest of all seeds. But if they are not mature, they are not even as good as the tares or weeds. With humaneness, too, maturity is everything."

10] Mencius said, "When Yi[12] taught people archery, he was always determined to draw the bow to the full, and the students necessarily did the same. When the master carpenter instructs others, he always uses the compass and the square, and the students necessarily use the compass and the square as well."

12. Yi was known as the greatest archer of antiquity.

BOOK 6B

[6B1] A man from Ren asked Wuluzi, "As between the rites and food, which is more important?"

"The rites are more important."

"As between sex and the rites, which is more important?"

"The rites are more important."

"If by observing the rites of eating one will die of starvation, while by not observing them one is able to eat, must one still observe the rites? If the requirement that one go in person to meet his bride means that he cannot get a wife, while not observing that requirement means that he can get a wife, must he observe the requirement?"

Wuluzi was unable to reply, so the next day he went to Zou to consult Mencius.

Mencius said, "What problem could there be in answering these questions? If you do not measure a piece of wood from the bottom but only see that it is aligned at the top, then a piece an inch square can be made to look as tall as a towering pavilion. Gold is heavier than feathers, but could this apply to a single clasp of gold and a cartload of feathers? If one takes a case in which eating is important, while observing the rites is not important, why stop with saying that eating is important? If one chooses sex as important and the rites as not important, why should one stop with saying that sex is important?

"Go and respond to him, 'If by twisting your brother's arm and snatching away his food you were able to eat, but by not snatching it you would be unable to eat, would you snatch it away? If by scaling the wall of your neighbor on the east and dragging off his daughter you could get a wife, while by not dragging her off you could not get a wife, would you then drag her off?'"

2] Cao Jiao asked, "Is it true that all human beings are capable of becoming a Yao or a Shun?"

Mencius said, "It is true."

"I have heard that King Wen was ten feet tall, while Tang was nine feet tall. I am nine feet four inches tall,[1] and yet all I can do is eat millet. What shall I do to become a Yao or a Shun?"

"What is there to do but just to do it? Here we have a man who is not strong enough to lift a chicken; he is a man who lacks strength. If he now says that he can lift a hundred *jun*, he is a man of strength, for by lifting Wu Huo's burden one becomes Wu Huo.[2] Why should one regard not yet having mastered something as a calamity? It is just that one has not done it. To walk slowly behind an older brother is called fraternal; to walk quickly ahead of an older brother is called unfraternal. Is there anyone who is unable to walk slowly? It is just that he does not do it. The Way of Yao and Shun was that of filial and fraternal duty, that is all. By wearing the clothes of Yao, speaking the words of Yao, and performing the actions of Yao, you become Yao. By wearing the clothes of Jie, speaking the words of Jie, and performing the actions of Jie, you become Jie."

Jiao said, "If I can get to see the ruler of Zou, I may be able to ask him for a house where I may live. I should like to stay here to receive instruction at your gate."

"The Way is like a great road. It is not difficult to know it. The failing people have is simply that they do not seek it. If you, sir, will go back home and seek it, you will have more than enough teachers."

3] Gongsun Chou asked, "Gaozi[3] said, 'The "Xiaopan"[4] is the poem of a small man.'"

Mencius said, "Why did he say that?"

---

1. Obviously, the Chinese foot was considerably shorter than the Western measurement; there is no clear scholarly consensus on how long it was in this time and place.

2. Wu Huo was a legendary strong man.

3. Mengzi's disciple. See 2B13, note 23.

4. Ode 197 (Legge, *Chinese Classics*, 4:336–40).

He said, "Because of its tone of resentment."[5]

Mencius said, "How narrow-minded was Old Gao in his interpretation of poetry! There is a man here. A man of Yue draws his bow to shoot him. Were I to talk of this in a jocular manner, it would be solely because he is not a relative of mine. But if my older brother were to draw his bow to shoot him, I would shed tears when telling of it solely because he is my relative. The resentment in the "Xiaopan" is an aspect of the intimacy one feels with one's parents, and intimacy with one's parents is humaneness [*ren*]. How narrow-minded Old Gao was in his interpretation of poetry.

"Why is there no resentment expressed in the 'Kaifeng'?"[6]

"In the 'Kaifeng,' the fault of the parent was small, while in the 'Xiaopan' the fault of the parent was great. When one is unresentful despite the fact that a parent's fault is great, the sense of estrangement is deepened. When one is resentful despite the fact that a parent's fault is small, an unwarranted obstacle is created. To deepen estrangement is to be unfilial and to create an obstacle is also unfilial. Confucius said, 'Shun was consummately filial, yet at the age of fifty he still longed for his parents.'"

[6B4] Song Keng was about to go to Chu when Mencius met him at Shiqiu and asked, "Where are you going, sir?"

"I have heard that Qin and Chu are at war, and I am going to see the King of Chu to persuade him to put a stop to it. If the King of Chu should not be amenable, I shall go to see the King of Qin to persuade him to put a stop to it. With two kings I shall surely have some success."

"I do not presume to ask about the details, but I would like to hear about the crux of the matter. How will you persuade them?"

---

5. Actually, Gongsun Chou's response to Mencius's question is just one word: *yuan* 怨, suggesting both sorrow and a sense of having been wronged. One interpretation of the poem is that it represents the lament of Yijiu, the oldest son and heir apparent of King You, the last ruler of the Western Zhou. When his father became enamored of another woman, Yijiu's mother was demoted and Yijiu was passed over as heir apparent in favor of a son of the king's new favorite.

6. Ode 32 (Legge, *Chinese Classics*, 4:50–51). According to the "Little Preface" to the *Classic of Odes*, the widowed mother described in this poem would like to remarry, while her seven sons tactfully resist this inclination.

"I shall explain the unprofitability of war."

"Your intentions, sir, are great, but your argument is faulty. If you, sir, use profit to persuade the kings of Qin and Chu, and if the kings of Qin and Chu, being amenable to the idea of profit, stop their armies, the personnel of those armies will be delighted with the cessation of hostilities and amenable to profit. Ministers serving their rulers will be preoccupied with profit; sons serving their parents will be preoccupied with profit; and younger brothers serving their older brothers will be preoccupied with profit. Finally, rulers, ministers, parents, children, and older and younger brothers will abandon humaneness and rightness and encounter one another based on a preoccupation with profit. Whenever this has happened, loss has always ensued. If you, sir, rely on humaneness and rightness to persuade the kings of Qin and Chu, and if the kings of Qin and Chu, being amenable to humaneness and rightness, stop their armies, then the personnel of their armies will be delighted with the cessation of war and amenable to humaneness and rightness. Ministers serving their rulers will be preoccupied with humaneness and rightness; sons serving their parents will be preoccupied with humaneness and rightness; younger brothers serving their older brothers will be preoccupied with humaneness and rightness. Rulers, ministers, parents, children, and older and younger brothers, abandoning profit, will encounter one another based on a preoccupation with humaneness and rightness. Whenever this has happened, the ruler has become a true king.[7] Why must you speak of 'profit'?"[8]

B5] When Mencius was living in Zou, Jizi, acting on behalf of the lord of Ren, sent him a present of silk, which he received without reciprocating. When he was living in Pinglu, Chuzi, who was a minister of Qi, sent him a present of silk, which he received without reciprocating. Later, when he was going from Zou to Ren, he met with Jizi, but when he was going from Pinglu to Qi, he did not meet with Chuzi. Wu

7. Unfortunately, the translation fails to preserve a Mencian play on words. Mencius has said that, when profit is central, the result is loss (*wang* 亡, in the second tone). When humaneness and rightness are central, the result is the rise of a true king (*wang* 王, in the fourth tone).

8. Compare with 1A1.

Luzi was happy and said, "I have gotten an opening."⁹ He asked, "Master, when you went to Ren, you went to see Jizi, but when you went to Qi, you did not go to see Chuzi. Was this because Chuzi was only a minister?"

"No. It says in the *Classic of Documents*, 'Along with the offerings there are many courtesies. If the courtesies do not measure up to the thing being offered, one must say that no offering has been made. This means that one has not exerted one's will in making the offering.'¹⁰ In this sense the offering is not complete."

Wu Luzi was pleased, and when someone asked him about this, he said, "Jizi could not go to Zou, but Chuzi could have gone to Pinglu."

[6B6] Chunyu Kun¹¹ said, "One who puts reputation and service first acts in the interests of others, while one who puts them last acts in his own interests. You, Master, were among the Three Ministers of the state, yet you departed before your reputation and service had reached to the ruler above or the people below. Is this really what a humane person is like?"

Mencius said, "Living in a lowly position, unwilling to dedicate his abilities to the service of one who was unworthy—this was Boyi.¹² Going five times to Tang, and five times to Jie—this was Yi Yin.¹³ Not disdaining to serve a sullied ruler, nor rejecting a minor post—this was Liuxia Hui.¹⁴ While these three masters did not follow precisely the same way, they were as one in terms of direction. What was that direction? It was humaneness. All that is expected of noble persons is that they should be humane. Why must they all be the same?"

---

9. Literally, "a crevice"—that is, a point of entry for discovering something about Mencius's priorities.

10. "The Announcement Concerning Lo," *Classic of Documents*, in Legge, *Chinese Classics*, 3:441.

11. Chunyu Kun was a native of the state of Qi. He seems to have had a special interest in needling Mencius. See also 4A17.

12. For Boyi, see 5B1.

13. For Yi Yin, see 5B1. Apparently, after he heeded Tang's call to come to serve, he paid the five visits to Jie, the "bad last ruler" of the Xia, in an attempt to assist him in reforming.

14. For Liuxia Hui, see 5B1.

Chunyu Kun said, "At the time of Duke Mu of Lu,[15] Gongyizi[16] was in charge of the government. Ziliu[17] and Zisi[18] were his ministers. Yet in the course of repeated attacks, Lu had its territory carved away, showing that those you consider worthy are of no benefit to the state."

Mencius said, "Yu did not employ Boli Xi,[19] with the result that the state perished; Duke Mu of Qin [659–620 B.C.E.] did employ him and, as a result, became hegemon. A state that does not employ the worthy perishes. How can the loss be limited to the carving away of territory?"

Chunyu Kun said, "Formerly, when Wang Bao[20] lived by the River Qi, the people in the area west of the Yellow River were good at ballads; when Mien Ju lived in Gaotang, the people in the area on the right of Qi[21] were good at songs. The women of Huazhou and Qiliang were so good at weeping for their husbands that they changed the customs of the state. What is present within must be manifested without. I have never seen one who performed some service without achieving a beneficial result. There must, therefore, be no worthy men. If there were, I would know about them."

Mencius said, "When Confucius was minister of justice in Lu, his advice was not followed. Then at a sacrifice the roasted meat was not brought to him. He left without taking off his ceremonial cap. Those who did not know him supposed that it was because of the meat. Those who did know him supposed that it was because it had not been a proper ceremony. Actually, Confucius wanted to take some minor offense as a ground for leaving. He did not want to leave for no reason at all. The actions of a noble person are certainly beyond the understanding of ordinary people."

15. Duke Xian (409–375 B.C.E.).
16. Also known as Gongyi Xiu, he was prime minister of Lu.
17. Also known as Xie Liu. See 2B11.
18. Or Kong Ji, who was Confucius's grandson.
19. For Boli Xi, see 5A9.
20. According to Zhao Qi, Wang was a talented singer from Wei. Zheng Zhen, in the *Chaojing chao wen ji*, cites a reference to Wang in the *Zuozhuan*, Duke Ai, sixth year, that he believes suggests that he was from Qi (Legge, *Chinese Classics*, 5:811).
21. That is, along the western borders of Qi.

[6B7] Mencius said, "The Five Hegemons[22] were offenders against the Three Kings.[23] Now, the several lords are offenders against the Five Hegemons, and the great officers are offenders against the lords. The Son of Heaven's visits to the lords were called tours of inspection [*xun shou*]. The lords' visits to the Son of Heaven were called reports on responsibilities [*shu zhi*]. In spring they observed the plowing and augmented any insufficiencies; in autumn they observed the harvesting and repaired any shortages.[24] If, when the Son of Heaven entered the borders, fields were being opened up, uncultivated lands reclaimed, the old nourished, the worthy honored, and the eminent placed in high positions, the lord was rewarded with land. If the Son of Heaven entered the borders and found land lying fallow and neglected, the old being abandoned, the worthy ignored, and the rapacious placed in high positions, the lord would be reprimanded. If a lord failed once to attend at court, he would be demoted in rank; for a second offense he would suffer a reduction of his landholdings; a third offense would result in armies moving in. Thus the Son of Heaven commanded the punishment but did not carry it out; the lords carried it out but did not command it. The Five Hegemons induced some of the lords to attack others, which is why I said that the Five Hegemons offended against the Three Kings.

"Among the Five Hegemons, Duke Huan[25] was most powerful. At the gathering in Kuiqiu,[26] the lords bound the sacrificial animal and made a document to record their agreement, but they did not smear their mouths with the animal's blood. The first injunction said, 'Punish those who are unfilial. Do not replace a designated heir, nor promote a concubine to the status of a wife.' The second injunction said, 'Honor

22. The Five Hegemons were Duke Huan of Qi (r. 685–643 B.C.E.), Duke Wen of Jin (r. 636–629 B.C.E.), Duke Mu of Qin (r. 659–620 B.C.E.), Duke Xiang of Song (r. 651–636 B.C.E.), and King Zhuang of Chu (r. 613–591 B.C.E.). Mencius regarded them as ethically inferior to true kings but not wholly without worth, as they preserved some vestige of proper hierarchy and order. See also 1A7, n. 19.

23. The founders of the Xia, the Shang, and the Zhou dynasties.

24. The lines beginning, "The Son of Heaven's visits to the lords . . . " and concluding " . . . in autumn they observed the harvesting and repaired any shortages" occur as well in 1B4.

25. Duke Huan of Qi.

26. Held in 650 B.C.E.

the worthy and nurture the talented so that Virtue may be made manifest.' The third injunction said, 'Show reverence for the old and compassion for the young. Do not be forgetful of guests and travelers.' The
fourth injunction said, 'Do not allow men of service to hold office on a
hereditary basis, nor one person to hold more than one office concur-
rently. In selecting men of service one must get the right ones. A lord
should not put a great officer to death solely on his own authority.' The
fifth injunction said, 'There should be no crooked embankments,[27] no
restrictions on the sale of grain, and no granting of a benefice without
this being reported.'

"They then said, 'All of us who have been allied through this covenant shall hereafter, in respect of this covenant, maintain good relations
with one another.'

"The lords of today all violate the five prohibitions, which is why I
say that the lords of today are offenders against the Five Hegemons.

"The crime of one who accedes to the wickedness of his ruler is small,
whereas the crime of one who incites the wickedness of his ruler is great.
The great officers of today all incite their rulers' wickedness. Therefore I
say, the great officers of today are offenders against the lords."

8] The ruler of Lu wanted to make Shenzi the commander of his army.
Mencius said, "To employ an uninstructed people in war is to bring
disaster upon them. Bringing disaster on the people was not accepted
in the time of Yao and Shun. Even if you could conquer Qi in a single
strike and capture Nanyang, it would not be right."

Changing countenance, Shenzi looked displeased and said, "This is
something I do not understand."

Mencius said, "I will explain it clearly. The land belonging to the
Son of Heaven amounts to a thousand square *li*. Were it not a thousand
square *li*, it would not be sufficient to allow him to host the lords. The
land belonging to a lord amounts to a hundred square *li*.

Were it not a hundred square *li*, it would not be sufficient to allow
him to preserve the important documents in his ancestral temple.

27. That is, no diversion of the water supply intended to advantage oneself at the expense of others.

"When the Duke of Zhou was enfeoffed in Lu, it was with a hundred square *li* of land. It is not that a hundred square *li* was insufficient, but it was limited to that size. When Taigong[28] was enfeoffed in Qi, it was also with a hundred square *li*. It is not that the land was insufficient, but it was limited to a hundred square *li*.

"Now, Lu is five times one hundred square *li* in size. Do you suppose that if a true king were to appear, he would bring harm or benefit to the state? If it were merely a matter of taking from one state in order to give to another, a humane man would not do it. How much less would he do it if his quest involved killing people? In serving his ruler a noble person focuses on guiding him along the right Way and committing himself to humaneness."

[6B9] Mencius said, "Those who serve the ruler today will say, 'We can enlarge the lord's territory and expand his treasuries and storehouses.' And, in the present age, for this they are called 'good ministers,' whereas in antiquity they would have been called 'thieves of the people.' To seek the enrichment of a ruler who neither follows the Way nor commits himself to humaneness is to enrich a Jie. Those who say 'We can form alliances with other states so that his military campaigns will be successful' are, in the present age, called 'good ministers,' whereas in antiquity they would have been called 'thieves of the people.' To bolster the military strength of a ruler who neither follows the Way nor commits himself to humaneness is to support a Jie. Even if he were to receive all-under-Heaven as a gift, one who follows the way of the present day without having changed present practices would be unable to dwell in it for the space of a single morning."

[6B10] Bai Kui said, "I want to set the rate of taxation at one part in twenty.[29] What do you think?"

Mencius said, "Your way would be the way of the Mo.[30] In a country of ten thousand households, would it be sufficient to have only one potter?"

---

28. Taigong, or Taigong Wang, was Lu Sheng, who assisted Kings Wen and Wu in the consolidation of the Zhou empire. See 4A13, 7A22, and 7B38.

29. By prevailing standards, a very low rate of taxation.

30. Pastoral peoples to the north. Legge and many other Western translators describe them as "barbarous tribes," which would seem to distort the sense in which Mencius referred to them.

Bai Kui replied, "It would not. There would not be enough vessels."

Mencius said, "Among the Mo the five grains are not grown; they grow nothing but millet. There are no walled cities, no stately dwellings, no ancestral temples, no rituals of sacrifice. There are no lords in need of gifts and entertainments, no hundred officers with their subordinates. Therefore, if they were to take one part in twenty, it should be sufficient.

"But we live in the Middle Kingdom. Are we to discard human relationships and dispense with nobility? Would that be acceptable? If a state cannot survive with only a few potters, how much less can it endure without nobility? If you wish to make taxation lighter than it was according to the way of Yao and Shun, you will be left with a greater Mo and a lesser Mo. If you want to make it heavier than it was according to the way of Yao and Shun, you will be left with a greater Jie and a lesser Jie."[31]

11] Bai Kui said, "When it comes to water control, I am better than Yu."

Mencius said, "Sir, you are mistaken. Yu's control of water followed the Way of water. Therefore, he channeled it into the four seas, whereas you, sir, channel it into neighboring states. When water overflows its course, it is called a deluge, and a deluge is a flood—something that a humane man detests. Sir, you are mistaken."

12] Mencius said, "If a noble person is not resolute, how will he exert control?"

13] The ruler of Lu wanted to have Yuezhengzi assume control of government. Mencius said, "When I heard of this, I was so delighted that I could not sleep."

Gongsong Chou asked, "Is Yuezhengzi strong?"

Mencius said, "No."

"Does he have sound judgment?"

"No."

---

31. If the rate of taxation is too light, civilization may not be sustained. If it is too heavy, exploitation cannot be precluded.

"Is he widely knowledgeable?"

"No."

"Why, then, were you so delighted that you could not sleep?"

Mencius said, "He is a person who loves the good."

"Is it enough to love the good?"

Mencius said, "To love the good is more than enough for governing all-under-Heaven. How should it not be enough for the state of Lu? If a minister loves the good, all within the four seas will consider a thousand *li* no great distance to come to report to him about the good. But if he does not love the good, people will say, "How arrogant he is! It is as if he knows it all already." Given the arrogance of his tone of voice and in his countenance, people will retreat to a distance of a thousand *li*. And when gentlemen retreat to a distance of a thousand *li*, those given to slander, fawning, and flattery arrive. He may still wish to see the state well governed, but, while surrounded by those given to slander, fawning, and flattery, will he be able to accomplish this?"

[6B14] Chen Zhen[32] asked, "What conditions did the noble persons of antiquity attach to serving in office?"

Mencius said, "There were three circumstances in which they accepted office and three in which they left it. When they were received with the utmost respect, in accordance with ritual, and told that the ruler would put their words into practice, they would remain. When the ritual courtesies were not yet dispensed with, yet their words were not being put into practice, they would depart.

"In the next case, although their words were not yet put into practice, if they were received with utmost respect, in accordance with ritual, they would accept office. But when the ritual courtesies were dispensed with, they would depart.

"The final case is that of the person who has eaten neither in the morning nor the evening. Hungry to the point of starvation, he is unable even to go out his door. Hearing of this, the ruler says, 'The great matter is that I am not able to put his Way into practice, nor am I able to follow his words. But I would be ashamed to let him die of starva-

32. A disciple of Mencius's. See 2B3.

tion in my domain.' In this case the assistance could be received, but only to the point of averting death by starvation."

5] Mencius said, "Shun emerged from the fields; Fu Yue was elevated from among the boards and earthworks; Jiao Ge from the fish and salt; Guan Yiwu from the hands of the jailer; Sunshu Ao from the seacoast; and Boli Xi from the marketplace. When Heaven intends to confer a great responsibility upon a person, it first visits his mind and will with suffering, toils his sinews and bones, subjects his body to hunger, exposes him to poverty, and confounds his projects. Through this, his mind is stimulated, his nature strengthened, and his inadequacies repaired. People commonly err, but later they are able to reform; their minds are troubled and their thoughts perplexed, but then they prove capable of acting. This becomes evident in their expressions, emerges in their voices, and, finally, they understand.

"Thus, in the absence of law-abiding families and worthy counselors within and hostile states and external challenges without, a state will often perish. From this we know that we thrive from experiencing sorrow and calamity, and perish from comfort and joy."

6] Mencius said, "There are many arts in teaching. If I decline to teach someone, I am teaching him all the same."

BOOK 7A

[7A1] Mencius said, "By fully developing one's mind, one knows one's nature. Knowing one's nature, one knows Heaven. It is through preserving one's mind and nourishing one's nature that one may serve Heaven. It is through cultivating one's self in an attitude of expectancy, allowing neither the brevity nor the length of one's life span to cause any ambivalence, that one is able to establish one's destiny."

[7A2] Mencius said, "There is, for everything, a destiny, but one should follow and accept only what is proper for oneself. Therefore, one who knows destiny does not stand under a wall in danger of collapsing. To die in the course of fulfilling the Way is a proper destiny, while dying in manacles and fetters is not a proper destiny."

[7A3] Mencius said, "If through seeking I get it while through neglect I lose it, such seeking is conducive to getting, for what I seek lies within myself. If, though my seeking is in accordance with the Way, yet getting depends on destiny, such seeking is not conducive to getting, for what I seek lies outside myself."[1]

[7A4] Mencius said, "All the ten thousand things are complete in me. To turn within to examine oneself and find that one is sincere—there is no greater joy than this. To dedicate oneself in all earnestness to reciprocity—there can be no closer approach to humaneness."

---

1. For another discussion of seeking (*qiu* 求) and getting (*de* 得), see 2A2.

5] Mencius said, "To carry it out without reflecting on it; to practice it without inquiring into it; to follow it over the course of a lifetime but not recognize it as the Way—this is the way with most people."

6] Mencius said, "A person must not be without shame. Shamelessness is the shame of being without shame."

7] Mencius said, "The sense of shame is of great importance to a person. One who is adept at clever schemes has no use for shame. If he is not ashamed that he is not like other people,[2] how can he become their equal?"

8] Mencius said, "The exemplary kings of antiquity loved goodness and forgot power. How could the exemplary scholars of antiquity have been any different? They delighted in the Way and forgot about the power of men. Therefore, if kings and dukes did not extend to them the utmost respect and observe the most complete propriety, they could not come to see them frequently, and if they could not come to see them frequently, how could they appoint them as ministers?"

9] Mencius said to Song Goujian, "Are you, sir, fond of traveling?[3] I will tell you about traveling: if some ruler recognizes your talent, be content; likewise, if none recognizes your talent, be content."

"What must one do in order to be content?"

"Honor Virtue and delight in rightness—this is the way to be content. Therefore, the scholar, however impoverished, never loses hold of rightness, and, however successful, never departs from the Way. Being impoverished yet not losing hold of rightness, the scholar keeps hold of himself. Being successful yet not departing from the Way, he never loses his capacity to inspire hope in the people. When the intentions of the men of antiquity were realized, they conferred benefits on the people. When they were not realized, they cultivated their own persons and

2. See 6A12.
3. Traveling to various courts to meet with rulers.

became known in the world. When impoverished, they cultivated their own goodness in solitude. When successful, they devoted themselves to encouraging the goodness of everyone in the world."

[7A10] Mencius said, "Not until a King Wen has appeared do ordinary people bestir themselves, whereas an extraordinary person bestirs himself whether or not there is a King Wen."[4]

[7A11] Mencius said, "One who had the wealth of the Han and Wei families[5] added to his own and yet regarded himself with a sense of dissatisfaction would have gone far beyond the average person."

[7A12] Mencius said, "If one employs the people in a way intended to ease their lives, though they may suffer, they will not be resentful. If one causes people's death in the course of trying to preserve their lives, though they may die, they will not be resentful of those who brought about their death."

[7A13] Mencius said, "Under the rule of a hegemon, the people look happy; under the rule of a true king, they look satisfied. If he kills them, they do not resent it; if he benefits them, they do not assign the credit to him. The people turn daily toward the good and do not know who brings this about. Where the noble person passes he transforms; where he resides he exerts a spiritual influence. Above and below, Heaven and earth, are all parts of the same stream. Can it be said that he adds but a small benefit?"

[7A14] Mencius said, "Humane words do not enter as deeply into a person's being as a reputation for humaneness. Good government does not work so effectively to deliver the people as good teaching. Good government inspires the people's fear, while good teaching inspires their love. Good government delivers the resources of the people, while good teaching gets their hearts."

---

4. See 7A22.

5. Commentators point out that the reference to "families" suggests that the reference must be to the Han and Wei families that were prominent in the state of Jin in the Spring and Autumn period rather than to the states of Han and Wei in the Warring States period.

[5]   Mencius said, "What people are able to do without having learned it is an expression of original, good ability. What they know without having to think about it is an expression of original, good knowledge. There are no young children who do not know enough to love their parents, and there are none who, as they grow older, do not know enough to respect their older brothers. To be affectionate toward those close to one—this is humaneness. To have respect for elders—this is rightness. All that remains is to extend these to the entire world."

[6]   Mencius said, "When Shun was living deep in the mountains, dwelling together with trees and rocks and wandering together with deer and swine, the difference between him and the rustic people who dwelled deep in the mountains was quite small. But when he heard a single good word or observed a single good action, it was like a river in flood or a spring flowing forth—nothing could contain it."

[7]   Do not do what you would not do. Do not wish what you would not wish. Only be like this.[6]

[8]   Mencius said, "Persons who possess the intelligence of Virtue and the skills of wisdom[7] are often those who have endured sickness and suffering. The solitary and unsupported minister or the concubine's son respond to danger by keeping control of their minds and become profound through anxiously anticipating calamities. Thus they achieve a penetrating understanding."

[9]   Mencius said, "There are people who serve a ruler for the sake of bringing pleasure to his countenance. There are ministers who would bring peace to the realm whose pleasure lies in pacifying the realm. There are the people of Heaven who apprehend what can be carried out throughout the world and then carry it out. There are the great persons who, through rectifying themselves, rectify all living beings."

6. For a fascinating discussion of this brief but intriguing and important passage, see David S. Nivison, "Problems in the Mengzi: 7A17," in *The Ways of Confucianism: Investigations in Chinese Philosophy*, ed. Bryan W. Van Norden, 167–73 (La Salle, Ill.: Open Court, 1996).

7. Following the reading of Zhu Xi.

[7A20] Mencius said, "The noble person has three delights, and being ruler over the world is not among them. That his father and mother are both alive and his older and younger brothers present no cause for concern— this is his first delight. That he can look up and not be abashed before Heaven, look down and not to be ashamed before others—this is his second delight. That he can get the most eminent talents in the world and educate them—this is his third delight. The noble person has three delights, and being ruler over the world is not one of them."

[7A21] Mencius said, "Extensive lands and a large population—the noble person wishes for these, but his delight does not lie in them. To stand in the center of the world and bring tranquillity to all the people within the four seas—the noble person delights in this, but that which he has as his nature does not lie in this. That which he has as his nature is neither increased through great actions nor diminished by living in poverty, because it is allotted to him. The noble person has as his nature humaneness, rightness, decorum, and wisdom, which, being rooted in his heart, grow apparent in the brightness of his countenance and the suppleness of his back and spread to his four limbs, in which are displayed a wordless illustration."

[7A22] Mencius said, "Boyi,[8] having fled from Zhou, was living by the shore of the northern sea. Hearing of the rise of King Wen, he bestirred himself[9] and said, 'Would it not be best to go back and follow him? I have heard that Xibo[10] is good at caring for the old.' Taigong,[11] having fled from *Zhou*, was living by the shore of the eastern sea. Hearing of the rise of King Wen, he bestirred himself and said, 'Would it not be best to go back and follow him? I have heard that Xibo is good at caring for the old.' If there were in the world one who was good at caring for the old, humane persons would all turn to him.[12]

---

8. See 2A2, 2A9, 3B10, 4A13, 5B1, 6B6, and 7B15.
9. See 7A10.
10. That is, King Wen.
11. See 4A13, 6B8, and 7B38.
12. The opening section of this passage is similar in content to 4A13.

"Around dwellings with five *mu* of land, mulberries were planted beneath the wall and were used by the women for silkworms, so that the old would have enough to dress in silk. With five brood chickens and two brood sows that were not allowed to miss their breeding seasons, the old would have enough so that they were not deprived of eating meat. And with the tillers cultivating their hundred *mu* of land, families with eight mouths to feed could avoid starvation.

"When it was said that 'Xibo is good at caring for the old,' what was meant was that he regulated fields and dwellings, taught people about planting and animal husbandry, and guided the women and children in taking care of the old. At fifty, people depend upon silk to be warm, and at seventy, they depend upon meat to be adequately nourished. To be deprived of warmth is called being frozen, and to be deprived of nourishment is called being famished. Among the people of King Wen, none were frozen or famished."

23] Mencius said, "Let their fields be well cultivated and their taxes be light, so that the people may be enriched. Let their foods be seasonable and their consumption according to ritual, so that their resources cannot be exhausted. Without water and fire, the people cannot live, but if you knock at someone's door at nightfall and ask for water and fire, there is no one who will refuse to give them, because they are so plentiful. A sage governs all-under-Heaven so that pulse and grain will be as plentiful as water and fire. When they are as plentiful as water and fire, how could there be any among the people who are not humane?"

24] Mencius said, "Confucius ascended the East Mountain, and the state of Lu seemed small. He ascended Mount Tai, and the world seemed small. Therefore, one who has looked at the sea finds it difficult to think of other waters, and one who has wandered within the gates of the sage finds it difficult to think of others' words.

"There is an art to looking at water—one must look at the waves, the form and appearance of which must be illuminated by the light of the sun or the moon. The flow of water is such that it does not move on until all the hollows in its course have been filled; the commitment of the noble person to the Way is not fulfilled until he has achieved a beautiful pattern."

[7A25] Mencius said, "One who rises with the cock's crowing and diligently devotes himself to goodness is a follower of Shun. One who rises with the cock's crowing and diligently devotes himself to profit is a follower of Zhi.[13] If you want to know what separates Shun and Zhi—it is nothing but the space between profit and goodness."[14]

[7A26] Mencius said, "Yangzi[15] chose egoism.[16] If by pulling out a single hair from his own body he could have benefited the entire world, he would not have done it. Mozi[17] chose impartial care. If by rubbing his whole body smooth from head to heel he could have benefited the world, he would have done it. Zimo held to the Mean, and by holding to the Mean he was closer to it. But holding to the Mean without allowing for exigencies resembles their holding to one point. The reason I dislike holding to one point is that one steals from the Way, holding up one point while suppressing a hundred others."

[7A27] Mencius said, "Those who are hungry find any food sweet, while those who are thirsty find any drink sweet. They are not able to get the true flavor of what they eat and drink because they have been injured by hunger and thirst. And is it only the mouth and stomach that are injured by hunger and thirst? The human mind may also be injured. A person who can prevent the injury caused by hunger and thirst from causing injury to the mind need not be concerned about measuring up to other people."

[7A28] Mencius said, "Liuxia Hui[18] would not have exchanged his sense of purpose for the three highest offices in the state."

13. The prototypical robber.
14. Compare with 1A1 and 6B4.
15. See also 3B9 and 7B26. Mencius's assessment of Yang Zhu's philosophy is extremely, and perhaps unfairly, critical. Unfortunately, there is no extant work by Yang Zhu or any record of his sayings that would allow a more objective judgment.
16. In Chinese, *wei wo* 為我, "for the sake of myself."
17. See also 3B9 and 7B26.
18. See also 2A9, 5B1, 6B6, and 7B15.

29] Mencius said, "One who has a purpose may be compared to one who is digging a well. To dig down seventy-two feet but stop without reaching the spring is like abandoning the well."

30] Mencius said, "Yao and Shun had them as their nature. Tang and Wu embodied them. The Five Hegemons made a display of them.[19] But displaying them for so long and not returning to their former ways, how could anyone know that they did not possess them?"

31] Gongsun Chou said, "Yi Yin said, 'I cannot stand by while someone goes against what is right,' and he banished Taijia to Tong. The people were greatly pleased. When Taijia became worthy, he brought him back. The people were greatly pleased. When a worthy person is serving as a minister for a ruler who is not worthy, can he banish him?"

Mencius said, "If he has the intentions of a Yi Yin, then he can. If he lacks the intentions of a Yi Yin, then it would be usurpation."

32] Gongsun Chou said, "It is said in the *Classic of Odes*,

He does not eat what he has not earned.[20]

How is it that the noble person eats though he does not plow?"

Mencius said, "When a noble person dwells in a state, and the ruler accepts his counsel, the result will be peace, wealth, honor, and glory. And if the young follow him, the result will be filial devotion, brotherliness, loyalty, and good faith. What better example of "not eating what one has not earned" could there be?"

33] The king's son Dian[21] asked, "What is the work of a scholar?"
Mencius said, "To exalt his intentions."

19. For the Five Hegemons, see 6B7, n. 22. The "them" in question refers to humaneness and rightness.
20. Ode 112 (Legge, *Chinese Classics*, 4:169–71). Legge and Dobson translate *bu su* 不素 as "does not eat the bread of idleness," drawing on the biblical book of Proverbs, but that seems slightly incongruous here.
21. Dian was the son of King Xuan of Qi.

"What do you mean by 'exalt his intentions'?"

"Being committed to humaneness and rightness, that is all. To put one innocent person to death contravenes humaneness. To take what is not one's own contravenes rightness. Where does he dwell? He dwells in humaneness. Where is his path? His path is rightness. In dwelling in humaneness and following the path of rightness the work of the great man is complete."

[7A34] If Zhongzi,[22] contrary to rightness, were to be offered the state of Qi, he would decline to receive it, and people would all believe his rightness to be exemplary. But this is the rightness of refusing a basket of rice or a bowl of soup.[23] Nothing a person does can be worse than abandoning his parents and relatives or the relation between ruler and minister, superior and inferior. How is it possible that one who displays small virtues can be credited with having great ones?"

[7A35] Tao Ying asked, "If, while Shun was Son of Heaven and Gao Yao was minister of justice, the Blind Man[24] had murdered someone, what would have happened?"

Mencius said, "Gao Yao would have apprehended him; that is all."

"But wouldn't Shun have prevented this?"

"How could Shun have prevented it? Gao Yao had received the authority for this."

"Then what would Shun have done?"

"Shun would have regarded abandoning the realm as he would abandoning an old shoe. Secretly, he would have taken his father on his back and fled, dwelling somewhere along the seacoast. There he would have happily remained to the end of his life, forgetting, in his delight, about the realm."

[7A36] As Mencius was going from Fan to the capital of Qi, he saw from a distance the son of the King of Qi. Sighing deeply, he said, "One's *qi* is

---

22. Chen Zhongzi appears in 3B10 as a person whose sense of rightness is, in Mencius's view, ostentatious but decidedly hypocritical.

23. See 6A10.

24. The "Blind Man" is Shun's father, Gusou (see 5A2).

influenced by the position one occupies, just as one's body is influenced by the nourishment it receives. Great is the influence of our position! Are we not all human in this respect?"

Mencius said, "The dwelling, the carriages and horses, and the clothing of the king's son are largely the same as those of other people, and his looking as he does is occasioned by the position that he occupies. How much more should this be true of one who occupies the wide house of the world!

"The ruler of Lu was going to Song, and he called out at the Tieze gate. The keeper of the gate said, 'This is not our ruler. Why does it sound so much like our ruler?' This is explained by the similarity of the positions they occupied."

37] Mencius said, "To feed someone but not to love him is to treat him like a pig. To love him but not to respect him is to make an animal of him. Honor and respect are what precede any presentation of gifts. There may be a show of honor and respect without any truth behind it, but the noble person cannot be retained through such pretense."

38] Mencius said, "Physical form and expressions belong to the nature endowed by Heaven. Only the sage is able to follow his physical form."

39] King Xuan of Qi wanted to shorten the mourning period. Gongsun Chou said, "To observe a single year's mourning is better than to dispense with it altogether."

Mencius said, "This is as if there were someone twisting his older brother's arm, and you said to him, 'Gently, gently,' whereas what you should be teaching him is filiality and brotherliness; that is all."

The mother of one of the king's sons died, and his tutor asked on his behalf if he could observe several months of mourning. Gongsun Chou said, "What do you think about this?"

Mencius said, "This is a case of wishing to observe the full mourning period but being unable to do so. Even if one adds a single day, it is better than dispensing with it altogether. I was speaking of a case in which, although there was no impediment, the mourning was not carried out."

[7A40] Mencius said, "There are five ways in which the noble person teaches others. One is by exerting a transforming influence, like a timely rain. One is by causing their Virtue to be fulfilled; one is by furthering their talents; one is by answering questions; another is by enabling them to cultivate and correct themselves on their own. These five are the ways in which the noble person teaches."

[7A41] Gongsun Chou said, "How lofty the Way is, and how beautiful! Indeed it is like ascending to Heaven—so attainable does it seem. Why not make it something that others might expect to attain in order to encourage them to make daily effort?"

Mencius said, "The great artisan does not change or dispense with the marking line for the sake of an unskilled craftsman, nor did Yi change his rule for drawing the bow for the sake of an inept archer. The noble person, having drawn the bow but not yet released the arrow, positions himself, as if by a great leap, at the center of the Way. Those who are able will follow him."

[7A42] Mencius said, "When the Way exists in the world, the Way must follow one's person. When the Way does not exist in the world, one's person must follow the Way. I have never heard of the Way following other people."

[7A43] Gongduzi said, "It would seem that when Teng Keng came to your gate,[25] it was an occasion for courtesy,[26] yet you never answered his questions. Why was that?"

Mencius said, "I do not answer the questions of one who asks presuming upon his status, his worthiness, his age, past services, or old acquaintances. In Teng Keng's case, two of these were applicable."

[7A44] Mencius said, "One who stops where stopping is impermissible will stop in anything he undertakes. One who is stingy with those with

---

25. That is, when he came to study with Mencius.
26. Teng Keng was a younger brother of the ruler of Teng. As Mencius explains, he refused to be swayed by, or even to respond to, persons who relied on status or connections.

whom he ought to be generous will be stingy with everyone. One who advances rashly will retreat hastily."

5] Mencius said, "The noble person loves living things without being humane toward them and is humane toward the people without being affectionate. That he is affectionate toward his family is what allows him to be humane toward the people and loving toward creatures."[27]

6] Mencius said, "There is nothing that the wise do not know, but what is urgent for them is confronting what is fundamental. There is no one whom the humane do not love, but what is fundamental for them is earnestly caring for the worthy. Even in the cases of Yao and Shun, their wisdom did not extend to everything, but they earnestly attended first to what was fundamental. The humaneness of Yao and Shun did not involve loving every person, but they earnestly cared for the worthy.

"To be unable to observe the three years' mourning while devoting scrupulous attention to the three months' mourning and the five months' mourning; to be gluttonous in one's eating and immoderate in one's drinking while inquiring about not tearing the meat with one's teeth—this is what I call 'not knowing what is fundamental.'"

---

27. Nivison points out an apparent connection between this passage and 3A5 ("On Translating Mencius," in *The Ways of Confucianism*, 196–97).

BOOK 7B

[7B1] Mencius said, "How inhumane was King Hui of Liang! The humane begin with what they love and proceed to what they do not love. The inhumane begin with what they do not love and proceed to what they love."

Gongsun Chou said, "What do you mean?"

"For the sake of territory, King Hui of Liang pulverized his people and propelled them into war.[1] In the wake of a great defeat, he engaged again, fearful he would not prevail. He importuned the son whom he loved until he buried him along with them. When I spoke of beginning with what one does not love and proceeding to what one loves, this is what I meant."

[7B2] Mencius said, "In the *Spring and Autumn Annals* there are no just wars. It does happen that some are better than others. 'Punishment' involves superiors attacking inferiors. Opposing states do not 'punish' each other."

[7B3] Mencius said, "It would be better not to have the *Classic of Documents* than to give it full credence. In the 'Completion of War,'[2] I find only two or three passages wholly credible. A humane person has no enemy in the world. When the one who was most humane attacked the one

---

1. Literally, he made an amorphous mass of them, as when rice is cooked down to make gruel. Rather than "propelled them into war," he "warred" them—"war" being used here as a transitive verb.

2. A part of the *Classic of Documents*. See Legge, *Chinese Classics*, 3:306–17. The chapter is an account of the final defeat of King Zhou of Shang by King Wu of Zhou and the submission of the people to King Wu.

most devoid of humaneness,[3] how could it have been possible that 'the blood flowed so that it floated the pestles of the mortars'?"[4]

4] Mencius said, "There are people who say, 'I am good at deploying troops, I am good at waging war.' This is a grave crime. If the ruler of a state loves humaneness, he will have no enemy in the world.

> When Tang pursued the work of punishment in the south,
> The Di in the north felt aggrieved.
> When he pursued the work of punishment in the east,
> The Yi in the west felt aggrieved, saying,
> 'Why does he leave us until last?'[5]

"When King Wu attacked the Yin, he had three hundred war chariots and three thousand fighters. The king said, 'Do not be afraid. I bring you repose. I am not an enemy to the hundred surnames.' The sound of people kowtowing[6] was like a mountain collapsing.

"To punish [*zheng* 征] is to correct [*zheng* 正]. With everyone wishing to be corrected, what is the need of fighting?"

5] Mencius said, "A woodworker or a wheelwright can give a person a compass and a square, but he cannot make him adept in the use of them."

6] Mencius said, "Shun, when he was eating dry grains or wild herbs, did so as if he would be doing so for the rest of his life. When he became

---

3. The one who was most humane was King Wu; the one who was least humane was the tyrant Zhou.

4. Legge, *Chinese Classics*, 3:315. Mencius's comment on this passage has occasioned controversy that has continued down the centuries. Both the *Classic of Documents* passage and Mencius's dismissal of it seem exaggerated. Can the war have been either as bloody as its author implies or as efficient as Mencius would have it?

5. Though the wording is slightly different, this quotation echoes the idea of "The Announcement of Zhong-hui" in the *Classic of Documents*. See Legge, *Chinese Classics*, 3:180–81.

6. Striking their foreheads against the ground as a gesture of respect.

Son of Heaven and wore embroidered robes, had a lute to play, and two women to serve him,[7] he did so as if they had always been his."

[7B7] Mencius said, "From this day forward I shall understand the weight of killing a person's relative. If you kill a person's father, that person may also kill your father; if you kill a person's older brother, that person may also kill your older brother. Thus, although you haven't done the killing yourself, it is just at one remove."

[7B8] Mencius said, "In antiquity, frontier stations were set up to prevent violence. Today they are established to create violence."

[7B9] Mencius said, "If a man himself does not practice the Way, it will not be practiced by his wife and children. If he does not employ other people according to the Way, he will not be able to employ it in regard to his wife and children."

[7B10] Mencius said, "A bad year cannot kill one whose store of grain is complete. A corrupt age cannot confuse one whose store of Virtue is complete."

[7B11] Mencius said, "A person who is fond of fame may be able to decline a state of a thousand chariots, but if he is not the person to do so, it will show up in his countenance even to decline a basket of rice or a bowl of soup."[8]

[7B12] Mencius said, "If the benevolent and worthy are not trusted, the state will be hollow and empty. If ritual and rightness are lacking, those above and those below will be thrown into confusion. If good governance is lacking, then resources will prove insufficient."

[7B13] Mencius said, "There have been cases where one who is not humane has gained control of a state but never a case where one who is not humane has gained control of all-under-Heaven."

---

7. The daughters of Yao. See 5B6.
8. For the example of the wayfarer and the beggar who refuse to accept food offered contemptuously, see 6A10.

14] Mencius said, "The people are of greatest importance, the altars of the soil and grain are next, and the ruler is of least importance. This is why one who gains the allegiance of the tillers of the fields will become the Son of Heaven, and one who gains the allegiance of the Son of Heaven will become one of the several lords, and one who gains the allegiance of the several lords will become a great officer. When one of the lords endangers the altars of the soil and grain, he is replaced. When the sacrificial animals have been perfect, the sacrificial vessels of millet have been pure, and the sacrifices have been timely, yet droughts or floods occur, then the altars should be replaced."

15] Mencius said, "A sage is the teacher of a hundred generations—so it is with Boyi and Liuxia Hui. Thus, when people hear of the character of Boyi, the corrupt become pure and the weak acquire determination. When they hear of the character of Liuxia Hui, the narrow-minded become liberal and the selfish become generous. They exerted themselves a hundred generations ago, and a hundred generations later all those who hear about them are similarly stirred. Had they not been sages, could they have exerted such an influence? And how much more did they affect those with whom they were personally associated?"[9]

16] Mencius said, "Humaneness is to be human. Spoken of collectively, it is the Way."

17] Mencius said, "When Confucius was leaving Lu he said, 'In time, in time, I shall depart.' This was the way to leave the state where his parents had lived. When he was leaving Qi, he strained the water off the rice that was to have been cooked and departed. This was the way to leave another state."[10]

18] Mencius said, "The reason Confucius was in distress between Chen and Cai was that neither their rulers nor their ministers communicated with him."[11]

9. See 5B1.
10. See 5B1.
11. See the *Analects* 11:2.

[7B19] Mo Ji said, "It is alleged that I speak very badly."

Mencius said, "There is no harm in that. The scholar dislikes confused talk. It says in the *Classic of Odes*:

> My anxious heart is full of trouble,
> I am hated by the herd of mean creatures.[12]

So it was with Confucius.

> Thus, though he could not prevent the rage [of his foes],
> He did not let fall his own fame.[13]

So it was with King Wen."[14]

[7B20] Mencius said, "It once was that the worthy would, through their own enlightenment, cause others to be enlightened. Now, there are those who try through their own benightedness to enlighten others."

[7B21] Mencius said to Gaozi,[15] "There are footpaths through the hills. If they are used, in short order they become roads. If they are not used, soon wild grasses will stop them up. Now wild grasses are stopping up your mind."

[7B22] Gaozi said, "The music of Yu was superior to the music of King Wen."

Mencius said, "On what basis do you say this?"

He said, "The knob on Yu's bell was worn through."

"Is that sufficient proof? Are the ruts in the road outside the city gate made by the force of just two horses?"[16]

---

12. Ode 26. Translation by James Legge (*Chinese Classics*, 4:39–40).

13. Ode 237. Translation by James Legge (ibid., 4:441).

14. In the context of the ode, however, it seems to have been said of the ancient Duke Danfu. See 1B5.

15. Mengzi's disciple. See 2B13, note 23.

16. The interpretation of this last sentence is much disputed. One interpretation has it that Mencius is suggesting that Gaozi failed to recognize that Yu's bell was much older than King Wen's and hence subject to greater wear. By analogy, more carriages would have arrived and departed just outside the city gates, which would have resulted in deeper ruts.

3] When Qi was afflicted with famine, Chen Zhen said, "The people of the state are all supposing that you, Master, will again request that the granary of Tang be opened for them, yet I am afraid that this may not be possible a second time."

Mencius said, "To do it would be to do a Feng Fu. There was a man of Jin named Feng Fu who was good at seizing tigers. Later, he became a good scholar. But when he went out to the wilds, there was a crowd of people in pursuit of a tiger. The tiger took refuge in a mountain, where no one dared attack him, but when the people saw Feng Fu, they ran and welcomed him. Feng Fu bared his arms and descended from his carriage. The crowd was pleased with him, but the scholars laughed at him."[17]

4] Mencius said, "The responses of the mouth to flavors, of the eye to colors, of the ear to sounds, of the nose to fragrances, and of the four limbs to comfort are our nature. But there is destiny in them, and the noble person does not call them 'nature.' Humaneness between parent and child, rightness between ruler and minister, propriety between guest and host, wisdom for the worthy, and the Way of Heaven for the sage are destiny. But our nature is in them, and the noble person does not call them 'destiny.'"

5] Haosheng Buhai asked, "What kind of a man is Yuezhengzi?"

Mencius said, "A good man, a trustworthy man."

"What do you mean by 'good' and 'trustworthy'?"

"The 'good' is what we may desire, and the 'trustworthy' is what we have within ourselves.

"When it is filled up within oneself, one may be called 'beautiful.' When it is filled up and brightly displayed, one may be called 'great.' When one is great and exercises a transforming influence, one may be called a 'sage.' One who is a sage and unknowable may be called a 'spirit.'

17. This would seem to have been a matter of credibility, in the manner of the fourth century B.C.E. Mencius evidently believed that his second request would be rejected and that, as a result, he would lose a measure of credibility, as did Feng Fu when he reverted to an earlier role of tiger tamer.

"Yuezhengzi is between the first two and the last four."

[7B26] Mencius said, "Those fleeing from Mo inevitably turn to Yang,[18] and those fleeing from Yang inevitably turn to us, the scholars. As they turn, they should simply be received. Today those who are disputing with the followers of Mo and Yang do so as if they were pursuing a stray pig. As soon as they have gotten it into the sty, they proceed to tie its legs."

[7B27] Mencius said, "Taxes are exacted in cloth, in grains, and in service. Of these, the noble person requires one and postpones the other two. If he requires two, there will be those among the people who die of starvation. If he requires three, fathers and sons will be separated."

[7B28] Mencius said, "There are three things that are precious to the lords: territory, people, and the affairs of state. One who values pearls and jade as precious must inevitably be visited by calamity to his person."

[7B29] When Pencheng Kuo took office in Qi, Mencius said, "He will die—Pencheng Kuo." When Pencheng Kuo was put to death, a disciple asked, "Master, how did you know that Pencheng Kuo would be killed?" Mencius replied, "He was a man with a modest amount of talent, but having never heard of the great Way of the noble person, it was just enough to get him put to death."

[7B30] When Mencius went to Teng, he lodged at the Upper Palace. A pair of sandals, not yet completed, had been left on the windowsill, but when the keeper came to look for them, they were nowhere to be found.

Someone asked Mencius, "Is this the way your followers go about concealing things?"

Mencius said, "Do you suppose that they came here to steal sandals?"

"Probably not," he said. "But though you, Master, provide instruction, you neither reprove those who leave nor reject those who come.

---

18. That is, the followers of Mo Di, the proponent of impartial care, and those of Yang Zhu, whom Mencius believed to be an egoist. See 3B9 and 7A26.

So long as they arrive with the mind to learn, you accept them; that is all."[19]

31] Mencius said, "All human beings have that which they cannot bear. Getting this attitude to reach to what they can bear is humaneness. All human beings have that which they will not do. Getting this attitude to reach to that which they will do is rightness. When human beings are able to bring to fulfillment the mind that desires not to harm others, their humaneness is inexhaustible, and when they are able to bring to fulfillment the mind that refuses to break through or to jump over a wall, their rightness is inexhaustible. If they can bring to fulfillment their reluctance to accept unsuitable modes of address,[20] there will be no place in which they fail to manifest rightness. If a scholar speaks of something about which he was not to have spoken in order to gain some advantage by speaking, or if he fails to speak of something about which he might have spoken in order to gain some advantage from not speaking, this is in both cases like breaking through or jumping over the wall."

32] Mencius said, "Words that are simple yet have far-reaching meaning are good words. What is simple to grasp and yet vast in its implications is a good Way. The words of a noble person do not go below the belt, but the Way is contained in them. The principles to which the noble person holds are for his own practice, but through them peace is brought to the world. The trouble with people is that they neglect their own fields while going to weed the fields of others. What they ask from others involves a heavy burden, while the burden they impose upon themselves is light."

33] Mencius said, "Yao and Shun had it as their nature; Tang and Wu returned to it. When every expression of one's countenance and every

19. Commentators differ over who is the speaker of these two sentences. If the received text is correct in referring to Mencius as Master (*fuzi* 夫子), then Mencius obviously cannot be the speaker. However, with a suggested variant, the text reads, "Now, I . . . " (*fu yu* 夫予), and Mencius is describing his pedagogical standards.

20. Literally, to be addressed as *er* 爾 or *ru* 汝, the former more informal and intimate, the latter a more formal and deferential word for "you."

movement of one's body is exactly in conformity with ritual, this is the ultimate in flourishing Virtue. Weeping for the dead should be out of grief and not for the sake of the living. Following the path of Virtue without deviation is not for the sake of an emolument. Speech must be trustworthy and not for the sake of acting correctly. The noble person carries out the law and awaits his destiny; that is all."

[7B34] Mencius said, "In advising great men one should regard them with disdain and not look at their grandeur. Lofty halls with soaring roofs and projecting rafters—were my wishes to be fulfilled, I would have none of this. Food spread out on vast tables with hundreds of servants waiting in attendance—were my wishes to be fulfilled, I would have none of this. A whirl of pleasure, a wash of wine, the rush of the chase, with a thousand chariots following along behind—were my wishes to be fulfilled, I would have none of this. What matters to great men is of no consequence to me. What matters to me are the standards of the ancients. Why should I be in awe of great men?"

[7B35] Mencius said, "To nourish the mind, there is nothing better than making the desires few. Here is a man whose desires are few; although there may be certain instances in which he is unable to preserve his mind, they will not be great in number. Here is a man whose desires are many; although there may be instances in which he is able to preserve his mind, they will not be great in number."

[7B36] Zeng Xi was fond of jujubes and Zengzi could not bear to eat them. Gongsun Chou asked, "Minced meat or jujubes—which is better?"

Mencius said, "Minced meat."

Gongsun Chou asked, "Why would Zengzi eat minced meat while refusing to eat jujubes?"

Mencius said, "There was a shared liking for minced meat, whereas the liking for jujubes was particular.[21] There is a taboo on the use of

---

21. Zengzi, missing his deceased father, could not bear to eat a food that had been a particular favorite of his father's, whereas eating a food that his father enjoyed in common with other people did not present the same problem of memory and longing.

a given name, but no taboo on the use of a surname.[22] A surname is shared, while a given name is particular."

7] Wan Zhang asked, "When Confucius was in Chen, he said, 'Would it not be better to return home? The scholars of my school are madly ardent and impetuous. Intent on going forward and seizing their opportunity, they do not forget their origins.'[23] Since Confucius was in Chen, why should he have been thinking about the mad scholars of Lu?"

Mencius said, "Since Confucius did not get those who followed the middle way, he had to accept the madly ardent and the cautiously restrained.[24] The ardent go forward and seize their opportunities; the restrained have things that they will not do. Confucius would have preferred those who followed the middle way, but, since he could not be sure of getting them, he thought in terms of the next best."

"I venture to ask what they were like—those who were called the 'madly ardent'?"

"Those whom Confucius called 'madly ardent' were such persons as Qin Zhang, Zeng Xi, and Mu Pi."

"Why were they called 'madly ardent'?"

"Their resolution led them to ostentatious invocations of 'The ancients! The ancients!' But, impartially assessed, their actions did not measure up to their words. When even the 'madly ardent' could not be found, Confucius wanted to get scholars who would not deign to involve themselves with anything impure. These were the cautiously restrained, and they were his next choice.

"Confucius said, 'When people pass my door without entering my house, it is only in the case of the village paragon that I feel no regret. The village paragon is the thief of Virtue.'[25] What sort of person was this that he could refer to as a 'village paragon'?"

"He is the sort of person who might say, 'Why are you so ostentatious? Your words are not supported by your actions, nor are your

22. There was a taboo on using the given name of one's deceased parent.
23. *Analects* 5:21.
24. *Analects* 13:21.
25. *Analects* 17:13.

actions supported by your words, yet you invoke "The ancients! The ancients!" Why are you so self-possessed, so cold? We are born into this world and must be of this world. It is quite enough simply to be good.' Eunuch-like, he ingratiates himself with a whole generation—such is the village paragon."

Wan Zhang said, "An entire village will praise this paragon; he is a paragon in everything he does. Why did Confucius consider him a thief of Virtue?"

"Blame him—you find nothing blameworthy. Reprove him—there is nothing to reprove. He conforms to prevailing customs; he harmonizes with an impure age. In his commitments, he seems loyal and trustworthy; in his actions, he seems incorruptible and untainted. The crowd is pleased with him, and he considers himself to be right. It is not possible to enter the Way of Yao and Shun together with him, and he was therefore called the 'thief of Virtue.'

"Confucius said, 'I dislike something that appears to be what in reality it is not; I dislike the weed for fear it will be confused with the grain; I dislike flattery for fear it may be confused with rightness; I dislike verbal facility for fear it may be confused with trustworthiness; I dislike the music of Zheng for fear it may be confused with authentic music; I dislike violet for fear it may be confused with vermilion; I dislike the village paragon lest his qualities be confused for Virtue.'

"The noble person turns back to an invariable regularity; that is all. The invariable regularity being correct, the multitudes will then be aroused, and when the multitudes are aroused, there will no longer be deviance and iniquity."

[7B38] Mencius said, "From Yao and Shun down to Tang was more than five hundred years. Yu and Gao Yao had seen Yao and Shun and knew them personally, while Tang had heard about them and knew them by reputation. From Tang down to King Wen was more than five hundred years. Yi Yin and Lai Zhu saw Tang and knew him personally, while King Wen had heard of him and knew him by reputation. From King Wen down to Confucius was more than five hundred years. Taigong Wang and Sanyi Sheng had seen King Wen and knew him personally, while Confucius had heard of him and knew him by reputation. From Confucius down to the present day has been more than a hundred years. We are so little removed from the time of the sage, and so close to the place where he dwelled. Is there then no one? Is there no one?"[26]

26. See 2B13.

GLOSSARY OF PERSONS AND PLACES

Bai Kui [6B10, 6B11].

Bi Zhan [3A3].

Bigan, Prince [2A1, 6A6].

Bin (state) [1B14, 1B15].

Biying [4B1].

Bo (state) [3B5, 5A6, 5A7].

Bogong Qi [5B2].

Bogong You [2A2].

Boli Xi [5A9, 6B6, 6B15].

Boyi [2A2, 2A9, 3B10, 4A13, 5B1, 6B6, 7A22, 7B15].

Cai (state) [7B18].

Cao Jiao [6B2].

Chang Xi [5A1, 5B3].

Chaowu (place) [1B4].

Chen (state) [7B18, 7B37].

Chen Dai [3B1, 3B10].

Chen Jia [2B9].

Chen Liang [3A4].

Chen Xiang [3A4].

Chen Zhen [2B3, 2B10, 6B14, 7B23].

Chen Zhongzi (Tian Zhong) [3B10, 7A34].

Cheng Jian [3A1].

Chess Qiu [6A9].

Chi Wa [2B5].

Chong (state) [2B14].

Chong Yu [2B7, 2B13].

Chu (state) [1A5, 1A7, 1B6, 1B13, 2B2, 3A1, 3A4, 3B5, 3B6, 6A4, 6A12, 6B4].

Chui Ji [5A9].

Chunyu Kun [4A17, 6B6].

Chuzi [4B32, 6B5].

Confucius [2A1, 2A2, 2A3, 2A4, 2A7, 2B13, 3A2, 3A4, 3B3, 3B7, 3B9, 4A2, 4A7, 4A8, 4A14, 4B10, 4B18, 4B22, 4B29, 5A4, 5A6, 5A8, 5B1, 5B4, 5B5, 5B7, 6A6, 6A8, 6B3, 6B6, 7A24, 7B17, 7B18, 7B19, 7B37, 7B38].

Dai Busheng [3B6].

Dai Yingchi [3B8].

Danzhu (son of Yao) [5A6].

Di (non-Chinese peoples) [1B11, 1B14, 1B15, 3A4, 3B5, 3B9, 7B4].

Dian (son of King Xuan of Qi) [7A33].

Ding, duke of Teng [3A1].

Dongguo family [2B2].

Duan Ganmu [3B7].

Fan (place) [7A36].

Fang Xun. See Yao.

Feilian [3B9].

Feng Fu [7B23].

Five Hegemons [6B7, 7A30].

Fu Chu [4B31].

Fu Yue [6B15].

Liang (state) [1A1, 1A2, 1A3, 1A4, 1A5, 1A6].

Ling, duke of Wei [5B4].

Lingqiu (place) [2B5].

Liuxia Hui [2A9, 5B1, 6B6, 7A28, 7B15].

Longzi (Master Long) [3A3, 6A7].

Lu (state) [1B12, 1B16, 2B7, 5B1, 5B4, 6B6, 6B8, 6B13, 7A24, 7A36, 7B17, 7B37].

Lu Shang (Taigong Wang) [4A13, 6B8, 7A22, 7B38].

Meng Ben [2A2].

Meng Jizi [6A5].

Meng Shishe [2A2].

Meng Xianzi [5B3].

Meng Zhongzi [2B2].

Mien Ju [6B6].

Min Zi [2A2].

Mingtiao (place) [4B1].

Mo Di (Mozi) [3B9, 7A26, 7B26].

Mo Ji [7B19].

Mo people [6B10].

Mount Chong [5A3].

Mount Liang [1B15].

Mount Qi [1B14, 1B15, 4B1, 5A6].

Mount Tai [1A7, 2A2, 7A24].

Mu, duke of Lu (Xian) [2B11, 5B6, 5B7, 6B6].

Mu, duke of Qin [5A9, 6B6, 6B7, 7A30].

Mu, duke of Zou [1B12].

Mu Pi [7B37].

Mu Zhong [5B3].

Nanyang (place) [6B8].

Ox Mountain [6A8].

Pencheng Kuo [7B29].

Peng Geng [3B4].

Peng Meng [4B24].

Ping, duke of Jin [5B3].

Ping, duke of Lu [1B16].

Pinglu (place) [2B4, 6B5].

Qi, viscount of Wei [2A1, 6A6].

Qi (son of Yu) [5A6].

Qi (state) [1A5, 1A7, 1B1, 1B2, 1B3, 1B4, 1B5, 1B6, 1B7, 1B8, 1B9, 1B10, 1B11, 1B13, 1B14, 2A1, 2A2, 2B2, 2B3, 2B5, 2B6, 2B7, 2B8, 2B9, 2B12, 2B13, 2B14, 3B5, 3B6, 3B10, 4A24, 4B31, 5A8, 5B1, 6B5, 6B8, 7A34, 7A36, 7B17, 7B23, 7B29].

Qi (Zhou territory in w. Shensi) [1B5].

Qiliang (place) [6B6].

Qin (state) [1A7, 5A9, 6A4, 6A12, 6B4].

Qin Zhang [7B37].

Qu (state) [5A9].

Ran Niu [2A2].

Ran Qiu [4A14].

Ran You [3A2].

Ren (state) [6B1, 6B5].

Robber Zhi [3B10, 7A25].

Rong (non-Chinese peoples) [3A4, 3B9].

Sanmiao people [5A3].

Sanwei (place) [5A3].

Sanyi Sheng [7B38].

Shang (Yin) dynasty [2A1, 2B9, 3A3, 4A2, 4A7, 5B4, 6B7, 7B4].

Shen Tong [2B8].

Shen Xiang [2B11].

Shennong [3A4].

Major Plays of Chikamatsu, tr. Donald Keene 1961

Four Major Plays of Chikamatsu, tr. Donald Keene. Paperback ed. only. 1961; rev. ed. 1997

Records of the Grand Historian of China, Translated from the Shih chi of Ssu-ma Ch'ien, tr. Burton Watson, 2 vols. 1961

Instructions for Practical Living and Other Neo-Confucian Writings by Wang Yang-ming, tr. Wing-tsit Chan 1963

Hsün Tzu: Basic Writings, tr. Burton Watson, paperback ed. only. 1963; rev. ed. 1996

Chuang Tzu: Basic Writings, tr. Burton Watson, paperback ed. only. 1964; rev. ed. 1996

The Mahābhārata, tr. Chakravarthi V. Narasimhan. Also in paperback ed. 1965; rev. ed. 1997

The Manyōshū, Nippon Gakujutsu Shinkōkai edition 1965

Su Tung-p'o: Selections from a Sung Dynasty Poet, tr. Burton Watson. Also in paperback ed. 1965

Bhartrihari: Poems, tr. Barbara Stoler Miller. Also in paperback ed. 1967

Basic Writings of Mo Tzu, Hsün Tzu, and Han Fei Tzu, tr. Burton Watson. Also in separate paperback eds. 1967

The Awakening of Faith, Attributed to Aśvaghosha, tr. Yoshito S. Hakeda. Also in paperback ed. 1967

Reflections on Things at Hand: The Neo-Confucian Anthology, comp. Chu Hsi and Lü Tsu-ch'ien, tr. Wing-tsit Chan 1967

The Platform Sutra of the Sixth Patriarch, tr. Philip B. Yampolsky. Also in paperback ed. 1967

Essays in Idleness: The Tsurezuregusa of Kenkō, tr. Donald Keene. Also in paperback ed. 1967

The Pillow Book of Sei Shōnagon, tr. Ivan Morris, 2 vols. 1967

Two Plays of Ancient India: The Little Clay Cart and the Minister's Seal, tr. J. A. B. van Buitenen 1968

The Complete Works of Chuang Tzu, tr. Burton Watson 1968

The Romance of the Western Chamber (Hsi hsiang chi), tr. S. I. Hsiung. Also in paperback ed. 1968

The Manyōshū, Nippon Gakujutsu Shinkōkai edition. Paperback ed. only. 1969

Records of the Historian: Chapters from the Shih chi of Ssu-ma Ch'ien, tr. Burton Watson. Paperback ed. only. 1969

Cold Mountain: 100 Poems by the T'ang Poet Han-shan, tr. Burton Watson. Also in paperback ed. 1970

Twenty Plays of the Nō Theatre, ed. Donald Keene. Also in paperback ed. 1970
Chūshingura: The Treasury of Loyal Retainers, tr. Donald Keene. Also in paperback ed. 1971; rev. ed. 1997
The Zen Master Hakuin: Selected Writings, tr. Philip B. Yampolsky 1971
Chinese Rhyme-Prose: Poems in the Fu Form from the Han and Six Dynasties Periods, tr. Burton Watson. Also in paperback ed. 1971
Kūkai: Major Works, tr. Yoshito S. Hakeda. Also in paperback ed. 1972
The Old Man Who Does as He Pleases: Selections from the Poetry and Prose of Lu Yu, tr. Burton Watson 1973
The Lion's Roar of Queen Śrīmālā, tr. Alex and Hideko Wayman 1974
Courtier and Commoner in Ancient China: Selections from the History of the Former Han by Pan Ku, tr. Burton Watson. Also in paperback ed. 1974
Japanese Literature in Chinese, vol. 1: *Poetry and Prose in Chinese by Japanese Writers of the Early Period*, tr. Burton Watson 1975
Japanese Literature in Chinese, vol. 2: *Poetry and Prose in Chinese by Japanese Writers of the Later Period*, tr. Burton Watson 1976
Scripture of the Lotus Blossom of the Fine Dharma, tr. Leon Hurvitz. Also in paperback ed. 1976
Love Song of the Dark Lord: Jayadeva's Gītagovinda, tr. Barbara Stoler Miller. Also in paperback ed. Cloth ed. includes critical text of the Sanskrit. 1977; rev. ed. 1997
Ryōkan: Zen Monk-Poet of Japan, tr. Burton Watson 1977
Calming the Mind and Discerning the Real: From the Lam rim chen mo of Tsoṇ-kha-pa, tr. Alex Wayman 1978
The Hermit and the Love-Thief: Sanskrit Poems of Bhartrihari and Bilhaṇa, tr. Barbara Stoler Miller 1978
The Lute: Kao Ming's P'i-p'a chi, tr. Jean Mulligan. Also in paperback ed. 1980
A Chronicle of Gods and Sovereigns: Jinnō Shōtōki of Kitabatake Chikafusa, tr. H. Paul Varley 1980
Among the Flowers: The Hua-chien chi, tr. Lois Fusek 1982
Grass Hill: Poems and Prose by the Japanese Monk Gensei, tr. Burton Watson 1983
Doctors, Diviners, and Magicians of Ancient China: Biographies of Fang-shih, tr. Kenneth J. DeWoskin. Also in paperback ed. 1983
Theater of Memory: The Plays of Kālidāsa, ed. Barbara Stoler Miller. Also in paperback ed. 1984
The Columbia Book of Chinese Poetry: From Early Times to the Thirteenth Century, ed. and tr. Burton Watson. Also in paperback ed. 1984
Poems of Love and War: From the Eight Anthologies and the Ten Long Poems of Classical Tamil, tr. A. K. Ramanujan. Also in paperback ed. 1985
The Bhagavad Gita: Krishna's Counsel in Time of War, tr. Barbara Stoler Miller 1986

The Columbia Book of Later Chinese Poetry, ed. and tr. Jonathan Chaves. Also in paperback ed. 1986

The Tso Chuan: Selections from China's Oldest Narrative History, tr. Burton Watson 1989

Waiting for the Wind: Thirty-six Poets of Japan's Late Medieval Age, tr. Steven Carter 1989

Selected Writings of Nichiren, ed. Philip B. Yampolsky 1990

Saigyō, Poems of a Mountain Home, tr. Burton Watson 1990

The Book of Lieh Tzu: A Classic of the Tao, tr. A. C. Graham. Morningside ed. 1990

The Tale of an Anklet: An Epic of South India—The Cilappatikāram of Iḷaṅkō Aṭikaḷ, tr. R. Parthasarathy 1993

Waiting for the Dawn: A Plan for the Prince, tr. with introduction by Wm. Theodore de Bary 1993

Yoshitsune and the Thousand Cherry Trees: A Masterpiece of the Eighteenth-Century Japanese Puppet Theater, tr., annotated, and with introduction by Stanleigh H. Jones, Jr. 1993

The Lotus Sutra, tr. Burton Watson. Also in paperback ed. 1993

The Classic of Changes: A New Translation of the I Ching *as Interpreted by Wang Bi*, tr. Richard John Lynn 1994

Beyond Spring: Tz'u Poems of the Sung Dynasty, tr. Julie Landau 1994

The Columbia Anthology of Traditional Chinese Literature, ed. Victor H. Mair 1994

Scenes for Mandarins: The Elite Theater of the Ming, tr. Cyril Birch 1995

Letters of Nichiren, ed. Philip B. Yampolsky; tr. Burton Watson et al. 1996

Unforgotten Dreams: Poems by the Zen Monk Shōtetsu, tr. Steven D. Carter 1997

The Vimalakirti Sutra, tr. Burton Watson 1997

Japanese and Chinese Poems to Sing: The Wakan rōei shū, tr. J. Thomas Rimer and Jonathan Chaves 1997

Breeze Through Bamboo: Kanshi of Ema Saikō, tr. Hiroaki Sato 1998

A Tower for the Summer Heat, by Li Yu, tr. Patrick Hanan 1998

Traditional Japanese Theater: An Anthology of Plays, by Karen Brazell 1998

The Original Analects: Sayings of Confucius and His Successors (0479–0249), by E. Bruce Brooks and A. Taeko Brooks 1998

The Classic of the Way and Virtue: A New Translation of the Tao-te ching *of Laozi as Interpreted by Wang Bi*, tr. Richard John Lynn 1999

The Four Hundred Songs of War and Wisdom: An Anthology of Poems from Classical Tamil, The Puṟanāṉūṟu, ed. and tr. George L. Hart and Hank Heifetz 1999

Original Tao: Inward Training (Nei-yeh) *and the Foundations of Taoist Mysticism*, by Harold D. Roth 1999

Printed in the USA
CPSIA information can be obtained
at www.ICGtesting.com
JSHW021101040823
45960JS00001B/15